Shakespeare in Kabul

Shakespeare in Kabul

Qais Akbar Omar
Stephen Landrigan

First published in Great Britain in 2012 by Haus Publishing Limited

HAUS PUBLISHING LTD.
70 Cadogan Place, London SW1X 9AH
www.hauspublishing.com

Copyright © 2012 by Qais Akbar Omar and Stephen Landrigan

print ISBN 978-1-908323-08-8
ebook ISBN 978-1-907822-48-3

Typeset in Minion by MacGuru Ltd
info@macguru.org.uk

Printed in Great Britain by the CPI Group (UK) Ltd, Croydon, CR0 4YY

A CIP catalogue for this book is available from the British Library

Contents

Resolution
(by Qais Akbar Omar and Stephen Landrigan)

for Elspeth Cochrane

In 2005, a group of Afghan actors performed William Shakespeare's *Love's Labour's Lost* in Kabul. It was the first time in nearly thirty years that men and women had appeared on stage together there. The world took notice. Nothing more poignantly captured the rising tide of optimism that was then sweeping post-Taliban Afghanistan.

Directed by Paris-based actress Corinne Jaber, the actors had confronted a series of daunting challenges: the complex language of the play, their inexperience doing theatre, the unyielding pressure of living in a conflict zone. In the end, though, they created one of the most unlikely productions of Shakespeare ever, and, in its own way, one of the most successful.

Love's Labour's Lost was a bold celebration of a new Afghanistan that the actors believed was taking shape around them. Yet less than a year later, when they toured the production to Mazar-e-Sharif and Herat, they discovered that their expectations for the future were not shared by all Afghans.

In the disappointments and violence of the years that have followed, *Love's Labour's Lost* appears all the more remarkable. It has become emblematic of both an extraordinary moment of hope, and a fleeting glimpse of what Afghanistan may someday yet become.

And for the actors as they remain committed to their vision of that new Afghanistan, *Love's Labours Lost* was a critical first step on a journey of discovery that continues for them still.

This is their story.

Exposition

by Stephen Landrigan

1

Prologue

Kabul. March, 2005.

The late afternoon air was unusually soft for Kabul, especially in the garden where we stood. It was a few days after *Naw Ruz*, the Zoroastrian New Year that falls on the first day of spring. Almond trees were in bloom, and their delicate scent was complemented by an angled light sifting over a small mountain nearby.

It was a nobleman's garden, laid out a century and a half earlier. It nestled between the arms of a large, gracious mansion that embraced it on three sides. A high wall enclosed it on the fourth. A small landscape of terraces, balconies, small niches and grand staircases made it feel like a place where special things should happen.

Everything about the garden was in stark contrast to the street outside. We had walked up a steep, deeply rutted lane that was muddy with water from squatters' houses. Their drains emptied untreated into the street. We carefully watched where we put our feet as we sidestepped the streams of effluent and dodged the taxis that use the narrow lane as a shortcut. As we made our way up, bicycles and little kids raced down. Several women in blue or white *burqas* walked past, their hands tightly gripping those of young boys or girls on whose eyes they depended to see where they were going.

From below us, a rage of horn-blowing swept up from Salang Watt, one of Kabul's busiest streets. Buses, cars and pushcarts loaded with fruits and vegetables vied to inch forward. A police car with its siren blaring was as caught in the gridlock as the rest. Everyone was in a hurry to get home. Shops were clanking down their metal shutters. Youngsters were running to nearby bakeries to buy bread for their family's dinners. The *muezzins* in the mosques were calling for the evening prayers. The air was filled with smoke, dust, and the smell of sweat and open ditches.

Mud-brick walls rose up on either side of the lane as we climbed with no indication what lay within. Ahead of us, where the road swerved to the left, a small cemetery held a dozen graves marked by piles of stones and green flags fluttering in an early evening breeze. This place was once far out in the country; the dead had expected to rest in peace. But the city had engulfed them, and now even a small flat area next to the graves was crammed with vendors selling phone cards, chewing gum, cold drinks and cigarettes from carts called *karachis*.

Just before the cemetery was a large entry through the wall on our right. Its thick wooden door, unlike any of the others we had passed, was wide open. A small sign above it read: Foundation for Culture and Civil Society.

Now we were inside. The wealthy family who owned this house was living elsewhere, renting out their mansion to the *kharijees*, the foreigners, for large sums. In these post 9/11 days, Kabul had been filling up with foreigners from dozens of countries. They had come to Afghanistan to put it to rights. I was one of them. I had arrived a year before, knowing nothing about Afghanistan, but hoping to be helpful.

I was with Corinne Jaber. She had come to Afghanistan to visit a friend. It was her first trip here. We had met a few weeks before, and discovered that we had theatre in common. She was an actress living in Paris. I was a playwright who had lost heavily on a play I had written and directed at the Edinburgh Festival two years earlier. To pay off my backers, for whom the play's excellent notices were not enough, I had taken a job chronicling a U.S.-funded education programme in Afghanistan.

∾

Corinne and I had just returned to Kabul from the northern city of

Mazar-e-Sharif. We had gone there separately with different groups of friends to celebrate *Naw Ruz*, the traditional Afghan and Persian New Year that falls on the first day of spring.

By chance, we both had booked into the normally placid UNICA Guest House operated by the United Nations. We were part of a swarm of foreigners who crammed into the high-ceilinged rooms of its Edwardian-era mansion and the small lodges scattered around its gardens. A dozen languages could be heard at the large table where we dined together.

Everyone had stories to tell about their work and adventures in Afghanistan. Everyone saw good things ahead in 1384, as Afghans styled the new year by the Muslim calendar, even though the tradition of celebrating *Naw Ruz* extends back at least a millennium before Islam to the Zoroastrians.

A blind optimism had swept Afghanistan following its incident-free presidential elections six months earlier. After three decades of turmoil and war, Afghanistan was on the path to better days, and everybody knew it.

No one was more upbeat than Robert Kluijver, a Dutchman working as the director of the Foundation for Culture and Civil Society. He had come to Mazar to oversee a festival of music and poetry to mark *Naw Ruz*. The *Mulla-e-Gul-e-Surkh*, the Red Flower Festival, is named for the wild tulips that spring up all across Afghanistan in the weeks around *Naw Ruz*. They flourish in the dry, stony fields along the road between Kabul and Mazar. Barely taller than the span of a hand, these are the ancestors to all the tulips that have made fortunes for Dutch growers.

Robert prefers to enjoy the tulips in their homeland, rather than his. He is an adventurer, a multi-linguist and a scholar of Islamic culture. Fluent in Dari, one of the principal Afghan languages, he had spent time in Afghanistan years before, and came back soon after the Taliban were driven out in late 2001. He brought with him a strongly held belief that the arts would be essential in revitalising Afghanistan after decades of brutality and war.

High on his list was repatriating the Afghan legacy of the poet known as Rumi who was born a few miles west of Mazar in the ancient city of Balkh. Rumi's mystical verses have been embraced by peoples around the world. A centrepiece of the Festival was a celebration of Rumi's poems that Robert organised in the Governor's Residence with readings both in Persian by Afghans, and in English by American poet Coleman Barks.

The next day, Robert staged a concert honouring *ustads,* the masters of traditional music, including some who played the twangy, uniquely Afghan lute-like instrument known as the *rabab.* Their hypnotic performances were rooted in tribal rhythms that extend from the heart of Central Asia to the Indus River.

I was astonished by the breadth of the cultural expressions I was experiencing. Like most foreigners in Afghanistan, I was woefully ignorant of the local culture.

Between events, Corinne and I wandered around the historic sites in Mazar, bargained in carpet shops, visited the *burqa* market and found something unexpected at every turn in the road. West met East on the East's own terms, and we were totally seduced.

Thousands of Afghans come from all over the country to be in Mazar for *Naw Ruz.* The city was buzzing. The crowds in Mazar's street were welcoming. Everyone wanted to shake our hands. As soon as we shook one, twenty others would stretch towards us. Rock stars receive this kind of adulation. It was heady. And it went both ways, judging from the excited smiles on the Afghans' faces. They were yet more evidence of the euphoria that seemed to be part of everything happening in Afghanistan in those happy months.

At the centre of Mazar is the striking blue-tiled shrine that gives the city its name. It marks a grave said to be that of Hazrat Ali, the nephew and son-in-law of the Prophet Mohammed, peace be upon him. The shrine is especially venerated by the Faction of Ali, the Shi'a. But at *Naw Ruz,* sectarian divisions get submerged in the fervour of making a pilgrimage to a place considered sacred by all Muslims.

We visited the shrine for the first time at night. It was festooned with twinkling lights that to our amazement squeaked out digitally generated versions of "Jingle Bells" and "Santa Claus is Coming to Town." Those who had hung the lights presumably had no familiarity with the tunes.

We returned during the day to watch the hawkers selling cheap green, white and red paisley scarves to the pilgrims who would then brush them on Hazrat Ali's tomb in hopes of taking the blessings of that holy place home with them. Other pilgrims did the same with the nougat candies for which Mazar is noted. Those sesame-flecked sweets would be saved for special guests.

Along one of the iron fences that surround the large gardens of the shrine, several Jogee women, who are part of the great tribe known elsewhere as Roma, were begging from the pilgrims. Some gave generously. Those seeking divine favour may have felt that their chances would be improved by showing a little generosity themselves.

On the sidewalks in front of the fences, wizened men in faded clothes sat selling artefacts unearthed from a land abundant with items crafted over the past ten thousand years. With their faces framed by turbans and beards, they waited for the foreigners and hoped for a big sale. Though trading in antiquities is illegal, no one was bothering them.

On *Naw Ruz* itself, we stood at the gates of the shrine's rose-filled garden, engulfed in a crowd of devotees. They were determined to touch a holy banner, the *janda,* within minutes of its being raised on a pole next to the shrine. They expected to receive a special grace for doing so. As hundreds of seekers mobbed the gates and others tried to climb the fence, police whipped them with thick leather straps. The crowd took the lashes and showed no reaction other than utter determination to get inside.

A policeman saw us in the crowd, and tried to open a way for us. For him, we were guests in his country, and he instinctively sought to make us feel welcome despite the surge around us. But Corinne, the only woman in the crush, smiled a "thanks, but no thanks" toward him as we edged out of the mob and away from the shrine.

We left touching the *janda* for later, and headed instead off to Balkh to see what was left of the world where Rumi had grown up. He and his family had been forced to flee from that ancient city by the onslaught of Genghis Khan eight hundred years before.

We were taken there by a young Afghan named Qais Akbar Omar. I had met him a few weeks earlier at a Sufi event held in the old mud-brick fort in Kabul where he and his family lived. He was in Mazar visiting relatives for *Naw Ruz*, and had offered to be our guide.

Balkh is one of the oldest known urban centres, rivalling Damascus and Delhi in the numbers of centuries it has been populated. Thick walls with high towers still flank its south side. The remains of 14th century arches and mosques from the age of Tamburlaine rise at its centre. Around them, women in white *burqas* were streaming to the grave of a young woman poet from the 15th century, Rabia Balkhi, who died for love. The *burqas* floated out behind them as they walked. Mysteriously, a large white owl swooped from the top of the shrine, though it was midday.

Nearby, a large group of men gathered in a circle to dance the *atan,* a Pashtun warrior's dance propelled by the pounding of deep-throated drums. A dancing goat kicked up its heels beyond them. Everyone was celebrating. Everyone was happy. The horrors of so many years were being set aside at last.

I had seen the same exultation a few days before during a *buzkashi* match waged on an open ground about a mile south of the shrine. More than a hundred long-coated, broad-hatted, high-booted *chapandaz* sat astride massive, spirited horses that were as single-minded as their riders to challenge the others. Their goal was to grab a headless, hoofless goat from the ground, carry it to the far end of the field and back again, then fling it into a small circle near where they had started.

Many of the riders were likely to get whipped mercilessly by the others as they hung off the sides of their horses trying to get control of the goat and race away with it. *Buzkashi* is warfare by another name. Many of those in the fray had been part of the leadership of the Northern Alliance that had helped drive out the Taliban. In this new Afghanistan, they battled with the elation of men freed at last from the uncertainties of real war.

Around the perimeter of the *buzkashi* grounds, a crowd, mostly men, shouted and wagered furiously. Many owned a string of *buzkashi* horses which they watched closely through binoculars from the rooftops of their costly, imported SUVs. There is great poverty in Afghanistan, but there is also great wealth.

∽

Corinne had travelled to Mazar in a convoy of Sufis. In Mazar, the Sufis invited me to their *zikkur,* a prayer meeting full of haunting singing and unbridled emotion. Corinne had not been allowed to attend. Women never are. She was learning in a very personal way how restrictive life for women in Afghanistan still can be, despite many changes.

The Sufis were as insistent in their hospitality as everyone else we were meeting. They took us to their homes for meals in Mazar. At one of them, a Sufi healer cured me of a migraine headache that had been plaguing me for a couple of days. He swiftly drew a sharp cutlass across my closed eyelids as he recited verses form the Holy Koran. The headache was gone instantly.

When the Sufis invited me to drive back to Kabul with them, I readily accepted. I had flown to Mazar in a small plane that had struggled to clear the towering peaks of the Hindu Kush mountains. It was a nerve-jarring flight, and I was relieved not to be flying back. I was really enjoying the Sufis' company and the vibrant strain of Afghan culture that they embodied. I was pleased I was going to have a chance to extend my time with them. Also, Corinne and Qais were travelling with them, as well. We had become good friends by then.

The road out of Mazar unrolled for an hour across the southernmost expanse of the Central Asian steppe before turning south through a narrow defile in the first range of mountains. The Sufis chanted poems by Rumi, Hafiz and Khaja Abdullah Ansari. Their voices were sweet. From time to time, Qais would tell us what they were singing about. Every now and again he joined with them for a few verses.

A few hours later, as we crossed a stretch of low sandy hills, the engine seized up. We coasted down a long hill, and with amazing good fortune rolled into the yard of the only mechanic within thirty miles. Sufi power? While the mechanic squatted on the car's grill and pulled the engine apart, we had a couple of hours to drink tea and eat *kebab* at a ramshackle, mud-brick, modern-day caravanserai.

From the terrace where we sat, we saw many black, goat-hair tents of Kuchi nomads pitched along a river across the road. We saw unveiled Kuchi girls as they walked between the tents and the river to draw water in pots they were carrying on their heads. They were dressed in colourful clothes like some I had seen commanding high prices as folk art in the Covered Bazaar in Istanbul.

∾

By midafternoon, we were rolling again, switchbacking up the north slope of the Hindu Kush mountains. The Sufis' chanting resumed for a while. When it slacked off, the driver slotted a cassette of Indian music into the tape deck and pumped up the volume.

As we cruised along at the lower elevations, fruit trees were in bloom. Red tulips carpeted the rocky fields. Grey-green Russian willows were in leaf. Grapes were spreading new tendrils. But as we climbed, the farms were replaced by angular boulders piled on bare rock. When we reached above ten thousand feet, we suddenly came back into winter.

High-walled canyons of snow rose above us. In coming months, its melt water would be carefully channelled around the fruit trees and crops of the farms below, as it had in this dry land for centuries. But for us near the top of the mountains, as we approached the mile-high Salang Tunnel, it simply made us feel very cold.

The tunnel, we soon discovered, had become impassable. The single-lane roadway leading to it had become a seven-lane scrum as *buzkashi*-minded drivers all tried to enter the tunnel ahead of the others. The effect was total gridlock. We sat in place waiting for things to break. The Sufis told stories. Qais told jokes. The daylight faded. Police walked up and down between the cars shouting, but nothing moved.

One policeman angrily pulled open the door of a small red car in front of us from which great clouds of marijuana smoke had been pouring all afternoon. Our driver had opened his window a few times to relish the effects of secondhand smoke, but the air was just too cold to leave it open. The policeman yelled at the occupants. We waited for an arrest. Instead, he climbed into the car, and closed the door behind him. About a half an hour later, he emerged, smiling.

As night fell and the Sufis drifted off to sleep, Corinne and I talked about what we had seen, heard, smelled, tasted, and been astonished by during our few days in Mazar. Though neither of us spoke Dari or Pashto, let alone any of the other twenty or so Afghan languages, we had been spellbound by the cadences of the poetry we had heard. There had been so much of it, even here in the car. Afghans, we had noticed, would sit motionless relishing every word and inflection when someone was reciting poetry.

After about four hours, a policeman jumped into our car and appointed himself as our guide to get us through the jam. He perched himself halfway out the window opposite the driver, and brandishing a Kalashnikov he screamed at the cars ahead of us to pull over. They did, and before long we were at the mouth of the tunnel. He rode with us through its unlit, smoky length and halfway down the mountain. His shift was coming to an end, he explained, and he had needed a ride back to his base camp.

By then, a nearly full moon had risen. Corinne and I continued talking, cross-referencing what we were encountering in Afghanistan with other things we knew or had read about over the years. It was a way of making sense of what we had experienced, and finding a place for ourselves in it. We reached Kabul with more questions than answers, and the process of discovery ongoing.

⁓

Now it was a few days later, and we had come to the Foundation for Culture and Civil Society to meet Robert Kluijver on his home turf. He had returned from Mazar only the night before, worn out from running a multi-site festival in a place with few resources and minimal infrastructure. Yet he was thrilled by the wildly enthusiastic response that the musicians had received. This was especially true for the Pashtuns from the southern and eastern regions of Afghanistan who had been rapturously embraced by festival-goers in the Uzbek- and Turkmen-dominated north.

We were meant to be talking about some sessions that Robert wanted Corinne to hold with Afghan actors at the Foundation. But the conversation kept drifting back to Mazar.

The Foundation had become a gathering point for actors, poets, musicians and others who were trying to find their way back to a kind of normality. It housed a small library and frequently showed classic films from Europe and the United States. Nearly all those who gathered there were men. They had spent years – some, decades – with their lives on hold, either living in refugee camps in Iran and

Pakistan, or dodging rockets in Afghanistan. Now they were desperate to make up for lost time.

Some had started making video dramas. Others were launching careers as singers. None had the tools or support they needed. Some came to the Foundation looking for training or advice; others, because they had nothing else to do.

In the Afghan way, they wanted to learn everything they could about anything at all. They were especially keen to know about theatre. Some had been exposed to theatre at Kabul University before the civil war broke out in the early 1990s. Others, as refugees, had had a passing awareness of the flourishing commercial theatre in Tehran or the more nascent one in Karachi. Most of them, though, had only a vague idea of what theatre is. For them, theatre remained a great unknown that provoked intense curiosity.

Robert wanted the actors to hear from Corinne what actors do in other countries. Corinne was at the forefront of the Paris theatre scene. She had recently won France's top theatre honour, the Molière Award, as best actress for her work in a play about the Armenian genocide called *The Beast on the Moon* by Richard Kalinoski. The play had resonances with Afghanistan. Also, Corinne had worked for many years with the visionary British director, Peter Brook. Corinne had toured several countries in his epic production of *The Mahabharata*.

She had come to the Foundation this afternoon to work out details with Robert on what she would actually do with the actors. I was tagging along. I was curious to find out what kind of theatre was happening in Afghanistan, and who was doing it.

I was just beginning to venture beyond the near-monastic world of the project that had brought me to Afghanistan. When I could sneak past our well-meaning security guards, I relished exploring the narrow lanes of Kabul's oldest neighbourhoods on foot.

I was often aided and abetted in my escapes by one of the drivers who had wandered the world for seventeen years as a displaced person while Afghanistan was enmeshed in upheaval. He had lived in more than twenty countries and had taught himself nine languages ranging from Punjabi to Thai. His name was Ali Khan.

Ali Khan was always ready for the next adventure. Sometimes that meant taking me to have lunch with his family on a Friday, the

Muslim holy day. Other times, we headed into the dusty hills south of Kabul to kick back with his buddies, reggae blasting from his tape deck as we drove past the ruined palace of a dead king. It had been with the help of Ali Khan that I had slipped the suffocating security net on my job that day, and come to the Foundation.

∿

As we waited for Robert, Corinne and I stood in the Foundation's garden all golden in that light, ensnared in the enchantment spun by its roses, its grand arches and doorways, its terraces and balconies and broad stairs and narrow stairs and so many places for entrances and exits.

I said to Corinne, "We must do a show here." I spoke softly, as if afraid to disturb the lengthening shadows.

"Yes," she replied in a well-enunciated, deep voice close to whisper. And with the poetry of *Naw Ruz* so fresh in our minds, she added, "Shakespeare."

And that is how it started.

2

A Cry of Players

Kabul. March, 2005.

A few days later, Corinne met with the actors. She drew from the experience of Peter Brook who had toured Africa with a troupe of actors doing what he had called "carpet shows." They would arrive in a village, spread out a carpet and start to perform. The intention, Corinne explained, was to establish a sense of immediacy that eliminated barriers between actors and audience.

Robert arranged for a large Hazaragi *kilim* to be spread on the grass in the Foundation's garden. Its had squares like a crossword puzzle, but in bright oranges, deep reds and rich blues laid out in diamond and sawtooth patterns. Its flatwoven colours mimicked the geraniums and tulips around the borders of the garden. It looked old. Perhaps for a generation or more it had covered the floor of the Hazara family whose women had woven it.

The actors sat in a circle on the *kilim*, their shoes lined up neatly at its edge, absorbing every word that came from Corinne, "like dry spinach in water," one of them said later.

That *kilim* was subsequently used in every rehearsal and performance. It became an unofficial totem of all that followed. It had been woven by women whose names would never be known, and who probably never thought of what they were making as the great art that it is. It was just something that they knew how to do. So, too, with the actors. Art was not a prime consideration. Performing was something they knew how to do.

With Qais serving as an interpreter, Corinne introduced herself as she shook hands with the actors, all male. Several of them offered long and formal welcomes in the Afghan manner. They conveyed their eagerness to learn anything that she could teach them.

Corinne told them about her work. Then she asked about theirs. A few of them, they explained, had done some theatre in the years before the fighting had started in the 1970s. Most of their work, though, had been on television, or in the low-cost Dari- and Pashto-language video dramas that served up thrillers and sentimental stories to local viewers.

Afghans, they explained, have only a short theatrical tradition, if one does not count the theatre erected by Alexander of Macedon when his army occupied parts of Afghanistan after 330 BCE. In the far northeast of the country, Alexander built a city on the Amu Darya River to mark the border of his empire. The buildings included a classical, open-air Greek theatre. Parts of it remains in the place now called Ai Khanum. It is the eastern-most Greek theatre known to have been built.

In recent history, the first theatrical performances in Afghanistan, so far as anyone has documented, occurred in the 1920s during the ten-year, western-looking reign of Amanullah Khan. After his ouster, conservative elements repressed public performances for the next quarter century. Then during the three decades of prosperity under Zahir Shah who came to power in the 1950s, theatre arts were introduced at Kabul University. Several of the older actors seated with Corinne on the *kilim* had trained there in those days.

They had studied with teachers who had come from the United States, Europe and Turkey. Some of their colleagues had gone to those countries for advanced training. In the 1970s, the Germans built a fully-equipped modern theatre that still stands, though in partial ruin after having been hit several times by rockets that blasted holes in its roof. Nearby is the stadium where the Taliban executed adulterers and homosexuals by stoning as a kind of morbid entertainment of a different sort.

In the 1980s, the Russians had built a modern performing arts centre where, in Soviet style, theatre troupes drawn from members of the Kabul police and fire departments had performed. It, too, had suffered heavy damage during the fighting after the Soviets left in 1989. It subsequently became a wasteland haven for drug users.

∿

Corinne proposed a series of exercises to the actors, who eagerly agreed. I watched from one of the projecting terraces that make the garden so idyllic. It was like a box seat overlooking the *kilim* that had become their stage. I did not know the actors' names yet. Several of them, though, were quickly emerging as specific personages in my mind.

One was named Nabi Tanha. When Corinne asked the actors to impersonate animals, he slunk into the crawl of a lion, as if he had been raised in a pride. It was a telling choice. Nabi Tanha turned out to be a primal force among the actors.

Another was a distinguished-looking middle-aged man named Qader Faroukh. He had the gravitas of a prime minister and a voice to match. He did not need to pretend to be anything. He projected raw animal power behind a façade of calculating calm. A few years later, he portrayed a retired Afghan general in the film, *The Kite Runner*. He was well chosen for that part.

One guy wore a U.S. army jacket, and threw himself into his improvisations as if he were engaged in hand-to-hand combat. He rolled on the ground, made big gestures, was wide-eyed one moment, and terrifying the next. I did not speak Dari then, and had to listen closely to hear that his name was Shah Mohammed. Later, when I knew him better, he showed me a photo of himself taken during the Taliban time. Like all men in Afghanistan then, had sported a full beard and turban. But even with the requisite joyless Taliban expression, a natural affability radiated from his eyes.

An older man was small and quiet. He had an engaging smile. I would find out later that his name was Kabir Rahimi. When he was impersonating something with wings – a bird? a butterfly? a bat? – he affected a quizzical look as he sought somewhere to land, and then total contentment as he settled on his perch. It was all precisely rendered with an economy of movement.

As the introductions were being made, it became apparent that the actors fell into one of two factions. One was led by Nabi Tanha, the other by Qader Faroukh. When Nabi Tanha looked displeased about something, everyone in his faction followed suit, even if they were not sure why. The same seemed to be true of the other faction as well.

After only an hour, everybody had to go home. Clouds darkened the sky earlier than usual, and a chill wind was sliding off the small, steep mountain behind the Foundation. Someone turned on the lights that ringed the garden. Birds recently arrived with the spring were flying from tree to tree, looking for their nests. Everyone said their goodbyes, and made plans to meet again the next day.

Before they left, Corinne told the men, "Please bring some women tomorrow." Corinne was determined not to let Taliban values prevail. There was a great silence. We sensed that finding women was going to be a problem for them. They said they would try.

That evening, Corinne was exhilarated as she spoke about the actors. Their enthusiasm, their intelligence, their openness, their rich sense of humour, and, above all, their craving to learn had impressed her greatly.

Several times she mentioned Nabi Tanha's proclamation that "If you were with us for six months, we could challenge the whole country." Those were words that she could not ignore.

∾

The next day, they all came back. With them was a woman, though only one. Her name was Parwin Mushtahel. Short and matronly, she had large curls of auburn hair that constantly fought to dislodge her headscarf. She maintained both the headscarf and a quiet dignity even as she threw herself into the day's exercises.

Corinne took charge from the moment she arrived. She walked to the centre of the *kilim*, which awaited them again on the lawn, and told the actors to gather in a circle. She had devised a series of activities, she told them as they settled around her. Her years of projecting lines to upper balconies have endowed her with a voice that commands attention as it commands.

The Afghan men showed no discomfort at being ordered around

17

by a woman. Nor did they seem to care when, once inside the Foundation's gate, Corinne let her headscarf with its brightly coloured stripes drop to her shoulders. They had seen women without scarves before. They were educated. Many had wives who did not wear headscarves at home.

Qais put it this way: "Afghans will accept almost anything if they believe that we will learn something. We really don't care if it is from a *kharijee*, a man or a woman. We are thirsty to learn. Our thirst for learning is never quenched."

It was another raw day. Everyone was dressed in jackets and pullovers. Corinne was wearing a knee-length *chappan* she had bought in Mazar, and which was to become something of a uniform for her. Without her scarf, her thick, curly, black hair fell in masses around her face. When she moved her head, her hair amplified its motion. Though she was then forty, she had the smooth, soft skin of a much younger woman, and the fitness of an athlete. It is her profession to make people look at her. It was hard not to.

Corinne and the actors worked together for more than an hour against the chill wind and the sounds of trucks and donkeys from beyond the walls. She showed them techniques for stretching the body and strengthening the voice.

Corinne told them more about the plays that she had done. She also talked of Shakespeare, Molière, Shaw, and other foreign playwrights. Nabi Tanha and Qader Faroukh, who had both studied theatre at Kabul University, relished the opportunity to share what they knew about these writers after so many years of not even hearing their names.

Over the next couple of days, Corinne met several more times with the actors. On the next to last day, however, Qader Faroukh's group did not come. Qader Faroukh himself appeared, and told Corinne that he and his group of actors would not be able to participate further. He had just been contracted to do a series of short plays about democracy all over Afghanistan. He was under pressure to get the plays up and running in less time than he needed. In the Afghan way, he asked her permission to be excused from her sessions.

When Nabi Tanha saw him leave and learned why, a victorious smile spread across his face.

That day, Corinne suggested that the actors do some improvisations. Nabi Tanha volunteered to play the moon, and he asked the other actors to play the stars. Qais said later, "I couldn't make any sense of what they were doing, but when I looked at Corinne, she had a big smile. She asked me with her eyes what I thought. I shrugged my shoulders, not sure what to say, because what I was seeing was incomprehensible to me." The actors, though, were having a good time stretching their imaginations.

After a while, tea came out to the garden on large trays. Nothing can be done in Afghanistan without green tea. The *kilim* was transformed from a stage to a *chai khana*, a tea house. The actors busied themselves with the cakes and cookies that had come with the tea. After fifteen minutes, Corinne asked Qais to gather everyone so they could continue working.

He tried, but none of the actors paid any attention to him. In the highly stratified social norms of Afghanistan, a younger person is not in a position to tell an older person what to do. Qais was younger than most of them. He explained his problem to Corinne.

Corinne pulled him by the arm, and dragged him towards the actors "as if I were guilty of something," he joked later. She asked him to interpret. She said, "Guys, let's work on the improvisations now, and we will have more tea later." They all said, "Okay," but continued their chat while sipping their tea. Discussions that begin over a cup of tea can go on for days.

She repeated, "Guys, let's work now. It will get dark, and we'll have to stop. We will drink tea later, after we finish." This time she sounded more insistent. Again everybody said, "Okay," but carried on as before until Nabi Tanha happened to look at Corinne, and read the frustration mounting on her face. He clapped his hands authoritatively, and said in a loud voice, "Stop eating and drinking and chattering. Let's work!"

Immediately, everybody put down their half-drunk glasses of tea and half-nibbled cookies. At that moment, it became evident that for this group of actors there were going to be two people in charge. Over the next several months, the balance of power shifted back and forth between Corinne and Nabi Tanha in an unrelenting and unpredictable process that became a drama of its own.

∾

On the last day before she returned to Paris, Corinne decided to give some shape to the improvisations, to see if it were possible to harness the creativity they embodied. After the physical and vocal exercises, which the actors were now doing well, she had everybody improvise a scene from *A Midsummer Night's Dream*.

She chose the scene in which the workmen enact the story of Pyramus and Thisbe. With no text in Dari for them to consult, Corinne explained to them the basic outline of the long-told tale of forbidden love. Then she asked them to act it out, and improvise as they went.

The result was astonishing. To start, the men had no hesitation in playing the female parts. Kabir willingly covered his head with a scarf to become Thisbe. Another actor took on the role of the wall, and with his thumbs and forefingers formed a chink through which the pining lovers could speak. All of them showed an unhesitating readiness to get up and tell a story.

To keep the gender-bending balanced, Parwin was asked to play a man. With no hesitation, she exchanged her headscarf for one of the men's *pakhol* hats, and wrapped herself in a *patu*, a woolen shawl worn by men. When she spoke, she did so in a gruff, deep voice.

The actors seemed to have no problem understanding the complexity of *A Midsummer Night's Dream*'s play within a play. They performed it with enthusiasm. Then they did it again, with each actor taking a different role. Some of them had never heard of Shakespeare, but they all agreed that he had come up with an excellent story.

Corinne ended the workshops promising to come back. At that point she did not know when, how or for what purpose. But she had made a deep personal connection with the actors. They had clearly accepted her. Several times during the sessions, one or another of the actors would whisper to Qais to ask if Corinne were going to start a project with them. Qais did not know. Not even Corinne was sure what might come next.

Robert Kluijver was eager to have her return, and do something large-scale. But what? More workshops? A series of scenes? A full play?

The task was to find the right project to which these actors could relate both personally and professionally. And one that could be in some way meaningful in the new Afghanistan.

Corinne left for Paris with her imagination whirling.

3

Selecting a Play

Back in Paris, with the dust of Kabul still in her shoes, Corinne decided that it did not make sense to do anything less than a full production of a play. She felt that if she could move the actors from a first reading to a closing night, she could expose them to a range of experiences that would serve them well in the future. It was an ambitious notion.

Within days, she spoke with noted French theatre director Ariane Mnouchkine who has worked with theatre artists from around the world, and who had already been asked by Robert Kluijver to do workshops in Kabul that summer with young Afghan actors. The workshops would be part of a larger Afghan Theatre Festival that Robert was organising.

Corinne sent e-mails to me in Kabul reporting that she and Ariane talked at length about what sort of play should be performed. They agreed, she wrote, that the tradition of epic poetry in Afghanistan pointed towards one of the great poet-playwrights.

Ariane suggested *Tartuffe*, by Molière. Its exploration of the evils caused by greed would have made it unwittingly prescient of the corruption that was just then beginning to exert its crippling stranglehold on Afghanistan. Corinne went back and read the script, though she knew it well. She looked for resonances that connected the play with her impressions of Afghanistan and the actors she had met there. She did not find what she sought. She felt that the play lacked the force of Shakespeare. She wanted a play that could draw on the physical and emotional energy that she had seen the actors generate.

Before she had left Kabul, Corinne and I had talked about several of Shakespeare's plays. We had had brainstorming sessions on the upper terraces of an old fort where she had been staying. The fort had been designed to house the king's top minister, his *wazir*. With high terraces that gave sweeping views over Kabul, it was a place that encouraged big thoughts and grand plans. With a bottle of white wine obtained from an embassy, and some Italian cheese found who-knows-where, we spread a *sofrah*, an eating cloth, on the floor and the ideas tumbled out.

Corinne's first instinct was to do a play related to warfare and struggle. She felt the Afghans could unleash their own experiences, and bring a power that actors in gentler places could not.

The history plays were intriguing to her, especially *Henry V*. Its recounting of the beleaguered and outnumbered English at the battle of Agincourt offered a striking parallel to the outgunned Mujahedin who had driven the Soviets from Afghan soil, though admittedly with considerable help from the United States.

Richard II loomed with its delineation of how a civil war can erupt between rival warlords when the government is corrupt. *Macbeth* was another obvious contender with its factional plotting and counterplotting.

And even *Othello* made a certain amount of sense. The story of the smitten young woman who is awarded as a bride to a middle-aged war hero with whom her father is seeking an alliance is very Afghan. Maybe too much so. It might be seen by some as a caution-ary tale on the mistreatment of women as pawns in male power games. But there was a danger that Desdemona's murder might be considered to be entirely justified by those who had cheered the Taliban.

Comedies such as *Twelfth Night*, *All's Well That Ends Well* and *As You Like It* are filled with male-female interactions that could be problematic in performance. Things had changed in Kabul. The

Taliban had been driven out, at least for a while. But it was difficult to know where the limits lay on depicting the courtship rituals that were central to these comedies.

Cymbeline and *Pericles*, though considered 'comedies', both have elements that are very dark. And though Pashtuns claim descent from the Jewish tribe of Benjamin, and Kabul for centuries had a thriving Jewish community, the anti-Semitism embodied in Shakespeare's portrait of Shylock put *The Merchant of Venice* off limits.

Measure for Measure and *The Taming of the Shrew* are not funny in a country where many women continue to be treated badly. *Much Ado About Nothing* has an unsettling scene in which a young man, after professing passionate devotion to one young woman, quickly agrees to marry her cousin whom he has never met when the first woman is believed to be dead. That sort of thing happens frequently in Afghanistan.

As the roster of plays was reviewed, and the pros and cons of each were weighed, an extraordinary fact became clear: Shakespeare in his time was in many ways much closer in spirit to the current situation in Afghanistan than we Westerners are in ours. That strengthened our resolve to find a play that spoke to the actors and through them to an Afghan audience.

Two comedies kept surfacing as likely choices: *The Tempest* and *A Midsummer Night's Dream*.

With its emphasis on reconciliation and its extended opportunities for clowning, *The Tempest* seemed like a good fit. Corinne was drawn to its tale of a king's being deprived of his kingdom and forced into exile by treacherous nobles who are essentially just a bunch of warlords.

But there was a big problem. Prospero's daughter Miranda has never seen a young man, then falls in love with the first one she meets, and pursues him relentlessly. For a young woman in Afghanistan, never to have spent time with a young man is typical. Pursuing one is not. Many Afghan women have few opportunities to encounter men until they are married, often times to a total stranger.

Still, the questions the play raises about the human condition made *The Tempest* relevant to the healing process then at work in Afghanistan. Also, there were opportunities to do theatrical magic, transforming the storm at sea, for instance, into the kind of blinding dust storm that can sweep across Afghanistan and blot out the sun. Instead of a ship, Prospero's brother and his court could be travelling by caravan. *The Tempest* also offers many opportunities for music, which we agreed should be central to any production.

Corinne worried, though, that without exactly the right cast, *The Tempest* was filled with potential pitfalls. She had seen a range of abilities among the actors in her workshops. Perhaps Nabi Tanha, with his lithe agility, could be a good Ariel. Possibly a Hazara actor could be found to play Caliban. Hazaras have too often been relegated to the lowest kinds of jobs in Afghanistan owing to their status as a religious and ethnic minority.

The only actor she had seen whom she could envision as playing Prospero was Qader Faroukh. Perhaps she could work around his schedule as he worked on the plays about the parliamentary elections. Until that could be investigated, *The Tempest* was put to the side.

That left *A Midsummer Night's Dream*. The Pyramus and Thisbe improvisation during the workshop had shown how completely the actors could inhabit Shakespeare's rustics. But what about the four lovers who fall victim to enchantments cast on them by the fairies?

Afghan folk tales are full of *jinns* doing impish things. So a story dependent on magical intervention was no problem. But would Afghan audiences accept watching young men and women flitting about a wood near Athens unchaperoned, professing love? Also, would Corinne be able to find young actresses who were up to the task? She had seen no actresses apart from Parwin. Were there others?

∾

In her spacious loft in an old industrial building near the Père Lachaise cemetery, she kept thumbing through the plays. There was another comedy, one not so well known or frequently produced, which struck her as uncannily embodying many parallels with the Afghan situation: *Love's Labour's Lost*.

Like many of Shakespeare's comedies, it is actually two plays entwined in one. One is lowbrow, pun-filled and bawdy. It uses every stock comic character that has trod a stage since Plautus. They bear names like Moth and Dull. Their chatter is full of topical references that no one since the play's premiere in the 1590s has understood without the help of footnotes.

And then there is the second play, a kind of a morality play enacted by four men and four women who bear titles of nobility. They speak in some of the richest verse Shakespeare ever wrote. Their jokes evolve from within the play itself, from the characters and the situation. Hence there is little about the humour that is dated.

The dilemma the play addresses has haunting echoes of the Taliban. Four virtuous young noblemen vow to retreat from the world to fast, study and refrain from seeing women for three years. They are serious in their ambition to use this time to improve themselves intellectually and spiritually. One of them, a king, issues an order that "no woman shall come within a mile of the court on pain of losing their tongue." They sign a contract to confirm their vows.

Almost immediately, four young ladies from a neighbouring kingdom arrive. The rules of hospitality require that they must be received, just as in Afghanistan where the Pashtunwali code demands that hospitality be extended to anyone who seeks it, even a sworn enemy. Housing the ladies in the king's palace, however, would force the four noblemen to dishonour themselves by breaking their vows. A man without honour in Afghanistan is not a man.

The situation is explained to the young ladies who are then asked to reside in the palace garden in a tent. The garden of the Foundation struck Corinne as ideal for such a setting, with a Kuchi nomad tent set amid the rose bushes and pomegranate trees.

The ladies accept this rather ridiculous situation with a twinkle in their eyes. They sense that all four of the young men find them attractive. They retire to their tent while each of the men quickly start seeking ways to have amorous messages delivered to them, but without the other men knowing.

Each sends love letters or poems to his favourite among the ladies, but the messenger who delivers the letters and their responses mixes them up, and gives them to the wrong persons. The young men accidentally discover each other's secret yearnings.

They then decide that love is more spiritual than anything else they might study. So they set off to discover the women's secret feelings. But since the women know of their vow, and since honour is at stake, the men must go in disguise.

What follows is as predictable as it is hilarious. The women hear about the men's plan, and decide to disguise themselves as well. The men arrive and plead their troth only to discover that each is wooing the wrong lady. The utter embarrassment felt by the men leads to a level of honesty that allows a resolution to evolve.

The women do not yield to the men's desire to be wed on the spot. Rather, they impose on the men a year's delay, a time of chastity and reflection, after which, if the men's sentiments remain unchanged, the women will be willing to take the sacred vow of marriage with them. For the women of *Love's Labour's Lost*, the bride price they are demanding is total commitment on the part of the men.

Interestingly, the women are not merely ornaments, but are the ones who decide upon how and when they will get married, and all four young men accept the imposed conditions. So the play ends where it started, with the four young men going on a retreat, but now their motives have changed, and are much more genuine.

Corinne was drawn to *Love's Labour's Lost* immediately because the cast requires an equal number of men and women, quite unlike *The Tempest*. This demand would support her goal of getting women on stage.

∿

As the idea of doing *Love's Labour's Lost* was taking hold, questions swirled as Corinne tried to visualise a production.

The play would require lots of cutting, even within the story of the four men and four women. References to European historical or mythological figures such as Pompey and Hercules would be impossible for Afghans to understand. But by focusing on the four young men and four young women, along with a pair of servants, a script could be devised for about ten actors and have a running time of about an hour and a half.

In one scene, the men disguise themselves as Russians to court the women. Perhaps the actors could learn some Russian, and do the scene as a satire of the Soviet invasion of Afghanistan. That notion proved to be wildly uninformed, however, as became evident later.

As the ideas started to sift into patterns of what was possible and what was not, Corinne began to see specific contributions that she could make.

She had been involved in many experimental theatre experiences, such as a tour of the Israeli play *The Dybbuk* in India, where she also had given workshops. She had adapted a short version of Shakespeare's *Antony and Cleopatra* for seven actors. She had also created and directed a one-woman show, given workshops and done some teaching. But she had never done anything as big as what she was proposing, and in a language she did not speak.

Yet, working across linguistic and cultural lines did not faze her. She had been born in Munich to a German mother and a father from Syria. When she was a young child, her family immigrated to Canada, where she mastered English. Later, they returned to Germany. At eighteen, she took herself to Paris, learned French, became an actress, and soon found herself at the Bouffes du Nord working with Peter Brook and a company of actors from nearly every part of the world. What she was proposing to do in Kabul might have been seen as an impossible challenge by someone else, but for Corinne it was simply an extension of her life and her work.

∽

After she had been home for two weeks, she gave Robert Kluijver a call. That helped clarify many things. He confirmed that Qader Faroukh would be touring Afghanistan all summer with the democracy play, and thus would not be available at all. Exit Prospero. No *Tempest*. But Robert encouraged Corinne to do a full-scale production. He saw it as being an ideal headline event for his theatre festival.

Some of the other actors whom she had seen had signed on to be part of Ariane Mnouchkine's workshops in Kabul. Robert suggested that Corinne do her production later in the summer than first planned. That would allow the actors to complete their work with Ariane, and then be available for Corinne. But that timeline posed problems for Corinne, who would have to be home in Paris by early

September, both for work commitments and to get her two daughters started in the new school year.

With all that turning in her mind, she still had not decided which play to direct. In the end, she decided that she needed to go back to Kabul as soon as possible and lay out a range of options to the actors. There was no point in trying to do a play which they did not want to do. While she was there, she could see whether, in fact, there were any other women willing to be involved besides Parwin.

Still, *Love's Labour's Lost* was fast becoming the play she wanted to do. She read and reread a series of lines by a character named Biron, who is both the most poetic of the four young men in the play, and the most grounded. After the men have discovered that each has been seeking the favours of the women, Biron makes an impassioned speech on the folly of foreswearing the company of women. He says:

From women's eyes this doctrine I derive;
They are the ground, the books, the academes
From whence doth spring the true Promethean fire….

For where is any author in the world
Teaches such beauty as a woman's eye?…

But love, first learned in a lady's eyes,
Lives not alone immured in the brain;
But, with the motion of all elements,
Courses as swift as thought in every power,
And gives to every power a double power,
Above their functions and their offices….

From women's eyes this doctrine I derive:
They sparkle still the right Promethean fire;
They are the books, the arts, the academes,
That show, contain and nourish all the world.

"From women's eyes…" These words kept echoing in Corinne's mind. "From women's eyes…" She heard them as nothing less than a hymn to women, as she came to say many times afterward. And they set in motion events that lead to a resolution decided by women. The words were powerful. And she believed strongly that they needed to be heard in Kabul where very often the only part of a heavily veiled woman that can be seen are her eyes.

∾

Before she left Paris to return to Kabul, Corinne called on Peter Brook. She wanted to ask his advice on directing Shakespeare in a place like Kabul. He had spent several months in Afghanistan in 1979 filming *Meetings With Remarkable Men*, based on the book of the same name by G. I. Gurdjieff.

Then eighty years old with a crown of white hair encircling his head, the man who had dazzled and challenged the English-speaking theatre throughout the second half of the 20th century spoke to her in his soft voice.

His message was simple. He told her not to impose her ideas on the Afghans, but rather to listen to the actors and to take what they had to give her. It seemed like straightforward advice, but she had no way of knowing then just how hard it would be to follow, nor how much the Afghan actors had to give her.

4

Finding Funds

We started calling the project *Shakespeare in Kabul*. That explained what we proposed to do as completely as any three words could. But until we had some funds to make it happen, it was only just a good idea.

Money was freely flowing in Kabul in those days, as foreign governments and international organisations looked for ways to make Afghanistan stable. Strangely, there was very little coordination among these donors, except informally when their staffs met at the growing number of surprisingly good restaurants that were springing up around Kabul to cater to the foreigners.

One notable exception to this disorganisation, however, was the combined efforts of several donors two years earlier that had led to the creation of the Foundation for Culture and Civil Society. Several donors shared the belief that cultural and intellectual ferment are essential elements in any forward-moving society. In Afghanistan, where the Taliban had deliberately sought to stamp out any kind of public cultural expression, that need was especially important. The World Bank and George Soros' Open Society Fund got the Foundation up and running, and the United Nations and the European Union quickly became hefty contributors.

From his position as the director of the Foundation, Robert Kluijver knew many of the Kabul decision-makers for the large donors. He offered to help us approach them, and to have the Foundation manage any funds we received. That gave *Shakespeare in Kabul* instant credibility.

We quickly put together a proposal that confidently asserted that "a nation's cultural life is built over time by the accretion of artistic events. *Shakespeare in Kabul* will be among the first for the new Afghanistan." It stressed the importance to both performers and audiences of having men and women appear on stage together for the first time in decades.

We figured that we would need about $30,000. Robert and one of his Afghan colleagues, Timor Hakimyar, started circulating our proposal to the donors.

First on the list was the cultural arm of the British Foreign Office known as the British Council. In Afghanistan the British Council had funded a substantial English-language library at Kabul University, and smaller ones at universities in Mazar-e-Sharif and Herat. Hosting cultural events was part of the British Council's mandate. *Shakespeare in Kabul* seemed to be exactly the kind of activity they would want to support.

We spent an afternoon with Richard Weyers, then the British Council's Kabul director. He had been in Kabul for nearly two years, and had a deep respect for Afghan culture, especially for the Afghan passion for poetry. He enjoyed the ease with which Afghans slip a couplet or two from the great Persian and Pashto poets into any conversation.

Some of his programme planners from London were in Kabul that week to discuss how the British Council could be most effective in Afghanistan in the year ahead. Richard arranged for us to meet them. We outlined our plans, noting how many people we would reach, how the actors would benefit from the training they would receive, what we saw as our long-term impact – all the things that are important to donors.

The delegation from London listened intently, and asked good questions. "We're a shoo-in," we told ourselves.

Corinne was in Paris at the time, and had been talking with some of her theatrical colleagues about *Shakespeare in Kabul*, soliciting their ideas and support. One of them, a director named Vincent Desforges, immediately understood the value of what she was proposing to do. He gave her $6,500 to help make it happen. It was a huge boost to us psychologically, and demonstrated to other potential donors the viability of our project.

Then a few weeks later, against all expectations, the British Council programme managers in London regretfully informed us that they had turned us down. They admired our intentions, they said, but had concluded that in Afghanistan, where the needs were so great, their limited funds would be better spent in other ways. Their argument was hard to challenge. They were doing good work. But we were heart-broken

No one was more disappointed than Richard Weyers. He was about to move on to a new posting for the British Council in Uganda. He spoke enthusiastically about the ingeniousness of using one of Shakespeare's greatest achievements in poetic drama to connect with a society which valued poetry above all other art forms.

He carefully reviewed his budget, and identified several activities on which more funds had been allocated than had actually been needed, as often happens. By assembling some unused funds from here and a few more from there, he was able to identify $20,000 that he could commit to *Shakespeare in Kabul*. "If Shakespeare is going to be performed in Kabul," he told Robert, "the British Council should support it." And so, singlehandedly, he made *Shakespeare in Kabul* possible.

A few weeks later, the Goethe Institut, the German government's counterpart to the British Council, contributed an additional $3,000. Its director in Kabul, Norbert Spitz, explained that the Goethe Institut was deeply committed to cultural regeneration in Afghanistan.

We were ready to roll.

5

Making the Script

Kabul. May and June, 2005.

While the search for funds was underway, Corinne sent an e-mail from Paris noting her growing enthusiasm for *Love's Labour's Lost*. I found a copy of the play online, and spent a couple of hours snuggled into a two-foot deep window ledge at the old fort reading it.

This was my first encounter with *Love's Labour's Lost*. My first reaction was dismay. How could the play's convoluted Elizabethan wordplay, which barely made sense to me, a native English speaker, work in Dari? The humour was laboured, and probably funny only to English majors. And what about the sexy sub-plot involving "a country wench?" Sure, the Taliban were gone – or at least we thought so then – but the script had moments that fell far beyond accepted social norms.

Skype was beginning to be known in Kabul that year. With the help of its cost-free phone links, I was able to speak to Corinne at some length a few days later.

"Disregard all the subplots, and the puns, and all that stuff. Just focus on the four men and the four women," she told me through an echo on the line.

I looked at the play again, reading only those characters. Corinne was right. Their story was a play unto itself. Its connection to the subplots was only tangential. Shakespeare, like his spiritual heirs in Bollywood, created shows that worked on several levels at once. He juxtaposed high-minded poetic dialogue against slapstick and mugging to keep his diverse audiences engaged.

I had seen lots of Bollywood films since I had arrived in Kabul. And I had discovered that being able to speak knowledgeably about Bollywood luminaries such as Shah Rukh Khan or Rani Mukerji was a great way of making conversation with Afghans. Once the talk turned to the on-screen exploits of John Abraham or the off-screen love affair between Abhishek Bachan and his then-fiancée Ayishwarya Rai, formalities got nudged aside. The social temperature warmed. It was as if we were speaking of family members whom we all knew well and dearly loved.

Visits to Afghan homes often meant seeing music video loops of Kareena Kapoor or Preity Zinta dancing their way through songs whose words they were mouthing. Bollywood is a solidly ingrained cultural fact of Afghan life. The exaggerated acting styles of some of its leading stars are seen as a high standard of performance art, one which Afghan actors strive to imitate.

The great Bollywood dramatic films of recent years such as *Veer-Zahra*, *Devdas* and *Kal Ho Na Ho* had all used musical numbers as critical turning points in the plot. I wondered if there might be a way of interpolating similar large musical numbers into our script, much as Shakespeare himself did in many of his plays, including *Love's Labour's Lost*.

I started crossing out all the lines in the script we did not need. Of those that remained, the ones that were absolutely essential were clearly evident. Those that were not, I also cut. I read what was left several times. And cut some more.

I established a base of about 1,000 lines out of the original 2,785. I had a tight script that allowed the flexibility for both further cuts or restorations. I identified several places where Bollywood-style songs could comfortably be inserted.

For a couple of weeks, Corinne and I filled the internet with some of Shakespeare's finest verse as we shuttled my draft, her edits, my suggestions, her corrections, my insistences, her second thoughts, back and forth. A fine script emerged.

All my Bollywood moments had been cut. Corinne said she would rather keep the production entirely Afghan and include traditional Afghan music. I tried to argue with her about the centrality of Bollywood music to Afghan life, but I had to agree with her in principle that Afghan music should be given its place.

In actual fact, we were getting ahead of ourselves. Corinne still wanted to involve the actors in the choice of the play. But she felt that if we had a well-constructed script for *Love's Labour's Lost* to present to them, they could make a more informed decision about the play.

∼

Malcolm Jardine arrived in Kabul to take over the leadership of the British Council there. A friendly, bespectacled man with short hair and a strong Glaswegian accent, he completely supported the decision of his predecessor, Richard Weyers, to fund *Shakespeare in Kabul*. Like Richard, he had spent many years in Islamic countries, and understood the centrality of poetry to their cultures. Introducing the poetry of Shakespeare to Afghanistan made complete sense to him.

In the same week that Malcolm arrived, I read a news item about the death in Iran of Dr. Alaeddin Pazargadi. In recognition of his achievements as a poet and writer, a public funeral had been held for him in front of Tehran University where he had taught for many years. Among other things, the news report stated that he had translated all of Shakespeare's plays into Farsi.

Where could we get a copy of them, I wondered, or at least a copy of *Love's Labour's Lost*?

I spoke to my friend, Ali Khan. He had a relative who travelled back and forth to Tehran several times a year. Perhaps he could get us a copy. But the relative had just arrived back in Kabul with no plans for returning to Tehran any time soon.

I checked at Shah's Book Store in Kabul, the subject of the much fictionalised *The Bookseller of Kabul* by Åsne Seierstad. But Mohammed Shah primarily stocks books in English. He would be happy to order a copy in Farsi from Tehran, he said, but it would be hard to know when it would come. Certainly not soon.

Qais, meanwhile, went to the local Dari and Pashto bookstores in Shahr-e-Naw that are full of gilt-edged editions of the poetry of

Omar Khayyam and Hafiz. But he had no luck finding Shakespeare. He trawled through the open-air book bazaar in Deh Mazang, poking through dozens of kiosks set up there by bookselling squatters, but nobody had anything by Dr. Pazargadi.

Meanwhile, I learned more about Dr. Pazargadi. He had been born in Shiraz in 1913, where he was educated in local schools. From there he went to England where he studied first at Manchester, and then at Oxford from which he received a Masters degree in political science in 1937. Having studied a PhD in education in the United States, he returned to Iran, and had a long career teaching English language and literature at Tehran University.

Over the next fifty years, he worked tirelessly on translating the complete works of Shakespeare into Farsi. He also authored and translated more than one hundred and twenty other books including English translations of Imam Ali's *Nahj-ul-Balagha*, poems of the Iranian poets such as Farrokhi Yazdi, Parvin E'tessami, Baba Taher, Sa'di, Hafiz, and Omar Khayyam. It turns out that he was a poet in his own right, as well.

I felt cheated that I had not had a chance to meet him. It would have been a great privilege to discuss our notion of staging Shakespeare with him, and to hear how he had gone about translating the script. Even more interesting might have been to have heard his thoughts on recent Iranian history and its effect on cultural expression.

I mentioned Dr. Pazargadi to Malcolm Jardine. The news story about Dr. Pazargadi's death had not stated whether his Shakespeare translations had actually been published.

Malcolm contacted his opposite number at the British Council in Tehran. Unlike the United States, the United Kingdom had maintained diplomatic relations with Iran. A few weeks later, Malcolm heard back that all of Dr. Pazargadi's Shakespeare translations had indeed been published, and were available in a two-volume set. His colleague offered to send a photocopy of *Love's Labour's Lost*.

Nearly a month passed before the copy reached Kabul. It had to travel through a diplomatic pouch via London. By then Corinne had come back to Kabul. That allowed the two of us a chance to discuss our adaptation of the English text, but it would be weeks before we had a Dari version.

∽

While we waited for the arrival of Dr. Pazargadi's translation, I did some research on the possible availability of other Farsi versions. Iran shared Afghanistan's passion for epic poetry. Indeed, over the centuries the two nations had often been a single country. Two great heroes of Persian literature, Rostam and Sohrab, had actually lived in Sistan and Zabulistan, the latter which is now a part of the present-day Afghanistan.

Despite Iran's poetic legacy, it was not until 1900 that any of Shakespeare's plays appeared in Farsi. The translator, Hosseinqoli Saloor, produced a Farsi version of *The Taming of the Shrew*. But it was based on a French translation. He had been educated in France where the Iranian elite studied, and did not speak English.

In 1917, *The Merchant of Venice* was again translated from French; another version followed twenty-three years later, this time drawn from an Arabic version.

The first Farsi translation of Shakespeare directly from English was *Othello*, published in 1914 by the Oxford-educated Mirza Abolqassem Khan Qaragozlu, a counselor to the Shah. It started as a challenge, with several of Mirza's friends insisting that it was impossible to render Shakespeare's poetry in Farsi. It took Mirza several years to do so, but all eventually agreed that he had produced an elegant translation that indeed captured the meter and expressed the nuances of the original. It received considerable acclaim from Iran's literary and political elite.

Other translators tried their hand at *Hamlet,* or returned to *Othello* and *The Merchant of Venice.* Some claimed they worked from the English originals, but admitted that they had used versions in French, a language they knew better, to help get them over the hump of Elizabethan English. In recent decades, translator M. A. Behazin has published Farsi versions of a few of Shakespeare's plays, but in prose, rather than poetry.

None of them, however, had translated *Love's Labour's Lost* except Dr. Pazargadi. His translations of Shakespeare's complete works were taken directly from the English originals. His work is an extraordinary literary accomplishment, though largely unknown outside Iran.

∾

The day that Dr. Pazargadi's translation finally arrived in Kabul was for me a day of celebration. To my close friend and co-worker, Qaseem Elmi, whom I had deputised as editor-in-chief of the script preparation process, it was the beginning of a month-long nightmare.

I had presumed that Dr. Pazargadi's Farsi version would be immediately intelligible to Afghan Dari speakers. I had been led to understand that Dari was a simple variant of Farsi. Over the coming weeks, however, I was to discover how different the two languages really are, despite their common roots. Even a natural linguist such as Qaseem was sorely challenged trying to weave their strands together.

Qaseem had grown up in the Afghan refugee camps that engulfed the Pakistani city of Peshawar as the fighting in Afghanistan raged for decades. His family had fled Afghanistan when he was five, leaving behind a comfortable middle-class life in Jalalabad for the squalor of mud-brick-and-tarp shelters in the camps. With a Pashtun father and a Tajik mother, he had learned both Pashto and Dari as a toddler. In Pakistan, he picked up Urdu by listening to Pakistani television. In the mosque, he mastered enough Arabic to read the Holy Koran.

As a young teenager, he realised that those with English language skills got better-paying jobs. He had learned some English in school, but enrolled in English language classes to improve his schoolboy speaking skills. He was soon fluent. A few years later, he was teaching English and employed by CARE International, earning $100 a month and being the breadwinner for his family.

When we met, he and I were both working for a U.S.-funded programme that provided primary education to teenagers who had never had any formal schooling. Many had been refugees and had come back to Afghanistan only to find themselves excluded from the Afghan school system because of their age.

Qaseem was an enthusiastic supporter of the programme, which was educating 170,000 youngsters across Afghanistan. He and I chronicled its successes as it improved the students' lives, along with those of their families and their entire villages. It was a brilliantly successful programme. We were proud to be part of it, and it had helped forge a deep bond between us.

We shared an office in a sprawling 1960s house that served as our education programme's offices. We had large windows that looked out over the home of one of our neighbours, whose three-story house had no front wall. It had been blown off or collapsed during the fighting. It was like an open-fronted doll house where the dolls had come to life.

About once every six weeks, Qaseem rearranged the office furniture. His desk was now across the room facing mine. I handed the photocopy of *Love's Labour's Lost* to him as soon as it arrived from Tehran.

A few minutes later he held up the photocopies, and asked me, "What language is this?"

"Farsi," I said, perplexed. He looked at it again.

"Are you sure?" he asked.

"I thought you spoke Farsi," I queried.

"I do." He put the Farsi photocopies on my desk, and picked up the English version that I had attached to it, and read a few pages.

"That's the original," I explained.

Qaseem's brow furrowed. He took off his glasses, and looked at me, then put the glasses back on, and looked at the script. Without his glasses, he bears more than a passing resemblance to the young Elvis Presley.

"What kind of English is this?" he asked. "No wonder I can't make sense of it in Farsi."

A learning process had just begun. It would take as many forms as there were people participating in it. Starting with me.

What became evident to Qaseem in the coming weeks, and to the actors in the coming months, was that Dr. Pazargadi had used many archaic Farsi words to make the vocabulary of his translation as contemporaneous with Shakespeare's original language as possible. As a literary achievement, it was a milestone. As a script for our team in Kabul, it was a massive challenge.

Dari is an older version of the language that has been spoken throughout the Persian lands for some three thousand years. In Iran, where the Persian Empire emerged from the tribal homelands of the Pars people, the language expanded as it accumulated vocabulary from Arabic- and Turkic-speaking neighbours. With the arrival of Islam in Iran, the language began to be written in Arabic letters. Because Arabic does not have the letter 'P', the 'Parsi' language became 'Farsi.'

Qaseem decided that the first thing we needed to do was to hand the photocopy of the script over to a typist to enter it into the Farsi/Dari word processing programme we used to typeset the textbooks that our project published.

The typist took days and extra days, as Afghans say, because he could not read whole sections of the photocopy that had had not reproduced well. It had tiny print to start with, and was filled with all those unfamiliar words. And since the written versions of Farsi and Dari do not express all the vowel sounds of the spoken languages, a reader encountering a new word for the first time must become a kind of detective to figure out what it is. Several words like that in a single line in the hard-to-read copy could stop progress for hours as Qaseem and the typist puzzled over them.

We were saved on several occasions by one of our colleagues, Khan Mohammed Stanekzai, who was a Pashto translator for our educational programme. He is also a highly regarded Pashto poet. He is equally fluent in Dari, and his poetic sensibilities helped unravel many of the linguistic riddles that Dr. Pazargadi had unintentionally concocted.

Stanekzai would stand in our office with his head tilted to one side as he gazed at the ceiling. Short and slim with an untamed thatch of curly hair, his lips would move silently as he repeated the lines that Qaseem had just read to him. Slowly he would work his way through the conundrum they presented, and start speaking as if he were channeling Shakespeare or Dr. Pazargadi.

Stanekzai argued that we should consider translating at least half the script into Pashto, since it was one of the national languages of Afghanistan, and more people speak it than Dari. As a poet, he told us, he could ensure that the meters and subtleties of both Dr. Pazargadi's and Shakespeare's intentions were met.

It was an intriguing notion. Might some of the characters speak in Pashto, while others respond to them in Dari? That kind of linguistic ping-pong happened every day on the streets of Kabul.

Perhaps a character played by Shah Mohammed, though he is not a Pashtun, but looks like one and can speak good Pashto, should speak in Pashto. But did that mean that the part played by Nabi Tanha should be in Hazaragi, the Hazara dialect of Dari, because he looks Hazara? Should an ethnic Uzbek actor speak Uzbeki?

The issue was settled by the software in the computer. It could not easily mix the Dari and Pashto alphabets. Both are based on the Arabic alphabet, but Pashto has more letters. Also, it requires diacritical marks that Dari does not use.

Just as well, since Qaseem and the typist were slowly going mad working only in Dari. Many weeks later, during the rehearsal process as Qais worked with the actors to punch up the jokes, some Pashto expressions and exchanges found their way into the dialogue.

In retrospect, we perhaps made an error by not including more Pashto. The new Afghanistan would have to move beyond the ethnic fault lines of the past. Perhaps a deliberately multi-lingual script would have helped point the way. But probably it would not have been enough for one good Afghan friend of mine, who refused to come to the play. Though he had trained as a physician in the United Kingdom where his family lives, speaks English, Dari, Pashto and Urdu fluently, and has travelled widely internationally, he is a serious Pashtun nationalist. He could not bring himself to consider attending a play presented primarily in Dari.

∾

As the typist worked away, I suggested to Qaseem that he transcribe only the lines we were planning to use. Qaseem said that it would be impossible to figure out what we were keeping and what we were cutting unless we first had the entire script in Dari. That seemed like a lot of wasted effort, given that we were planning on cutting half of the script. But it proved to be a lucky break for us. Later, when we wanted to restore several lines that we had previously cut, we had them all in the Farsi/Dari master script.

I printed out a copy of the full text of the play in English, then drew blue lines through all the lines that we had decided to eliminate. The plan was for Qaseem to put the Dari and English texts side by side, synoptically, and go through the Farsi/Dari version drawing blue lines of his own where he saw lines had been cut in English.

It was a slow process. In Farsi and Dari, verbs typically are placed at the end of the sentence. Shakespeare places his verbs where he needs them to support the meter or to lend poetic grace. Qaseem was driven to distraction trying to sort them out. He had a Farsi dictionary on one side of his desk, and an English dictionary on the other. Frequently, he failed to find in either the 16th century words he sought.

Like many young Afghan men, Qaseem is a body builder. Several nights a week, he would head to a gym after work. As the translation process wore on, though, the gym visits decreased, and he stayed at the office working on the script long after office hours had ended. It was around that time that he started smoking. I have always felt as if I were an unwitting enabler to that dangerous and filthy habit.

As the translation process wore on, Qais started coming to our office and spending several hours each day with Qaseem finding ways to keep the poetry intact, even as they looked for ways of substituting Dari equivalents for unintelligible Farsi words. Qais by then was working with Corinne on the production.

How many words could they modernise before the rhythms of Dr. Pazargadi's verse were lost or the subtleties of Shakespeare's language became clouded? It was a delicate task. Stanekzai stood by, offering poetic suggestions. Discussions – conducted in three languages simultaneously – sometimes got heated. From time to time, one or another would stride out of the office, fed up. But no Afghan can stay out of a good fight for long. A few minutes later, with a cup of green tea in hand, he would come back in, determined to prevail.

Ironically, the lines that had been the hardest for the typist to decipher were in many cases those with the densest wordplays and scatological jokes that Corinne and I had axed. Labours lost, indeed. Qaseem drew blue lines through many of the typist's most agonised renderings, and fumed at the amount of time he and the typist had wasted trying to decipher the incomprehensible. Finally, with Stanekzai's help, Qaseem and Qais felt they had crafted the script that Corinne and I wanted – in a language that neither she nor I spoke.

Climax

by Qais Akbar Omar

6

Casting: The Boys

Kabul. May, 2005.

When Corinne first came to Kabul, she stayed at the old mud-brick fort called Qale-e-Noborja where my family had been living for sixteen years. We had come there as refugees during the war. Soon we would be moving back to our side of Kabul where we were building a house to replace the one that had been heavily damaged in the fighting.

The first time I met her, she was sitting on the floor in one of the largest rooms in the old fort. She was having a little floor picnic with the friend she was visiting. Several candles had been lit, and a small wood fire burned in the *bokhari* stove set up in front of a large window. The warmth from the fire was chasing away the chill of the late winter evening. A cloth had been spread with several things to eat on it. She offered me a cracker with a piece of cheese. She said she had brought the cheese from France. It smelled like stinky feet.

She was an actress, she told me. I asked her if I might see one of her movies. She explained that she did theatre, not films. That brought back a flood of memories from the old days when my father or one of my uncles used to take my cousins and me to Kabul Nandari where a theatre company put on shows. Sometimes in school we did little plays written by our teachers, mostly about teachers and students, or soldiers and their captain, or parents and children. We always had one to perform on special occasions such as Teacher's Day, Mother's Day, Women's Day or Afghanistan Independence Day.

In the days that followed, I took Corinne carpet shopping and to many other places in Kabul. We made several visits to a police station after her passport was stolen. I tried to answer all her questions about Afghans and Afghanistan. She told me that I was arrogant. I told her that she was bossy. We got along well.

We saw each other almost every day. When Stephen could sneak away from his job, we would all meet at one of the Afghan restaurants in Shahr-e-Naw Park and eat *kebab*. I had met Stephen only a few weeks before Corinne had arrived. We had all been in Mazar together, and had become good friends very quickly.

On her first visit to Kabul, Corinne had asked me to work with her if money could be raised to do a project. I had told her I would. Now she was back, and we were ready to start.

Robert Kluijver at the Foundation for Culture and Civil Society had me sign a contract that said I was the Assistant Director of *Shakespeare in Kabul*. That made it official.

Robert was one of the few foreigners who could speak Dari, and fluently. I was impressed by the way he used Dari slang. He spoke with the tip of his tongue. Who was this Afghan, I wondered, with his thick sandy hair, stunningly blue eyes, and pale skin who had been born in another country, and who was so very pleasant, always smiling, and could carry on a good conversation with several people about several different things at one time? He always had a joke and time for anybody who wanted to talk with him, especially Afghans. Not all the *kharijees* in Afghanistan have been so welcoming.

Sometimes he spoke to Corinne in French, though she speaks English fluently. She also speaks German, I discovered. I listened to them and could not make sense of a word of what they were saying. Are they telling each other secrets, I wondered? Perhaps Corinne thought the same when Robert and I spoke to each other in Dari.

∾

I had never been to the Foundation before we started our work on the play. Now, when I came through its entry hall from the dusty street and into its garden, I felt I was back in the Kabul of my grandfather, when the city was small, friendly, green with trees and aromatic with a hundred types of blossoms, especially roses.

Some rich man had built this house about a hundred years before. I am sure that he had had even more flowers then and more fruit trees, all kept in perfect order. Even now, though, with its slightly forlorn look, the garden was quickly becoming a place where my spirit could be at ease. On many days, I came early for our sessions so I could sit there by myself for an hour and imagine a time before the Russians, the Mujahedin, and the Taliban.

When it was built, this house was out in the country, a couple of miles from the Old City that rose across the Kabul River around the thousands-year-old citadel called the Bala Hisar. The house had been built on the lower slope of the antenna-crowned hill we now call TV Mountain. Below the mountain, the small Pashtun village of Deh Afghanan once spread over the land that is now Zarnegar Park.

A prince named Habibullah, who later became king, built a small palace nearby in the early 1900s. Other wealthy people followed. They probably had seen photos of European villas in magazines, and gave copies to their builders. Some of the houses look a little bit German, some look a little bit Italian. All of them, though, have a completely Afghan feeling in the way they are centred on their gardens.

We still have a handful of these mansions to remind us of the time when Kabul could be a place of comfort. The Foundation's house is one of the best.

∽

One day, soon after Corinne had arrived back from Paris, she gave me some papers. "I think this is going to be our play," she said. "*Love's Labour's Lost.*"

I did not know much about Shakespeare, except that he was an important English playwright and very famous worldwide. At Kabul University, we had read one scene from *Hamlet* in Dari. I wanted to read more. His work had a quality that excited me. I went to the Kabul University library where I found his complete works in English, but I did not know enough English then to understand the old words that he used. I looked for Dari translations. The closest I could find was *Othello* in Farsi.

From the moment I started reading the first page, I found it unlike anything else I had ever read. I "nailed myself to it," as we say in Afghanistan, and kept on reading. I missed lunch and was shepherded out of the library when it closed for the day. I went home, and continued reading until I finished it. I was not such a slow reader, but I had to hear every line in my mind, and turn over the meanings of all its words before I went to the next one. *Othello* is not a happy story, but I was exhilarated when I had finished reading it. I had been caught in the web of its poetry.

With these fond memories of *Othello*, I was eager to read *Love's Labour's Lost*, especially since Corinne had told me that it was a comedy. Reading it, however, was more work than fun. The copy she gave me was in Farsi, but that was not the problem. I had read hundreds of Iranian novels during Taliban time when we had had no TV for six years.

This Farsi version, though, had many old English words that were not even translated into Farsi, such as 'Duke.' I looked for 'Duke' in an Iranian dictionary, but did not find it. Suddenly, it crossed my mind to look for it in an English dictionary, and there it was. With the help of two dictionaries, I made my way through the play.

∽

I suggested to Corinne that we should change the play's setting to Afghanistan, and make Shakespeare's King of Navarre the King of Kabul. The ladies who come to visit should not be from the French court, but from Herat, a city with a long artistic and historic heritage. She agreed.

Corinne wanted to keep all the parts about romantic love, even though we do not have that in Afghanistan. We have arranged marriages, and if somebody feels romantic towards their husband or wife, they are very lucky. Romantic love is something we see in Indian movies, or read in novels, and hear about in the verses of our great poets.

I told her that we could not have any touching between the men and the women. The Afghan audiences would not be happy to see that, even though we like it when we see Indians doing it in films.

Shakespeare included a poetry competition, which we both wanted to keep. Poetry and competitions are both very Afghan. Indeed, when we have parties, we often have poetry battles.

In our version, *Love's Labour's Lost* starts when the King of Kabul walks into his garden and asks his three friends to sign a strict oath that for the next three years they will "not to see a woman…. one day in a week to touch no food, and but one meal on every day…to sleep but three hours in the night, and not to be seen to wink of all the day." The King wants his friends to devote themselves to study and self-improvement without the distractions of normal life.

We hoped that these first speeches would make many people laugh. But I worried that it would be a bitter laughter, because the oath would remind some in the audience of the Taliban's rules.

∾

No one in my family, neither on my mother's nor father's sides, had ever been involved with acting, movies or theatre. We had grown up watching Indian movies, of course, with all their songs and dances in unexpected moments and their emotional overacting. But watching was as close I got to them. Now, I saw myself as a part of that world, if only a very small part.

Corinne set up operations in a room at the Foundation in what had once been a grand salon. It had tall windows that overlooked the garden. A half-dozen actors showed up on her first day back. They were excited to be doing a project, even though Corinne had not yet told them exactly what she had in mind.

She told them that she wanted to do a play by Shakespeare, but did not mention *Love's Labour's Lost* by name. She had to be ready to do a different play in case she could not find enough actresses for *Love's Labour's Lost*. It really did not make much difference to the actors which play they did. They just wanted to perform.

Without explaining why she was doing it, she guided them through some improvisations based on the story of the four men in *Love's*

Labour's Lost. She would explain a scene for them, and then have them play it in different ways. It gave her a chance to see who could do what. The actors were excited, and responded enthusiastically to what she suggested.

In one of the improvisations, they decided to play the young men as Taliban. Corinne, like most foreigners, had the impression that the Taliban were holy men, even if they had some strange ways of being holy. The actors, however, presented them from an Afghan perspective.

Their Taliban were vulgar and illiterate, spitting on the floor and smoking, shouting at each other as they talked. They picked lice from their own legs or from each other's, and did a lot of scratching. Corinne and I laughed and laughed. The more she laughed, the more outrageous the actors became. We learned two things that day: the actors were very good comedians, and they knew how to work an audience – even an audience of two – to milk a response.

Three of the actors were emerging as probably the best choices to play the nobles in *Love's Labour's Lost.* One was Nabi Tanha, who had a commanding presence, both on stage and off. Another was his sidekick Shah Mohammed Noori who was very dignified and energetic. A third was their frequent collaborator, Faisal Azizi, a young actor with a natural gift for comic timing. Also, the older actor, Kabir Rahimi, had a smiling buoyancy that would be ideal for the pivotal role of the servant who carries messages between the men and the women and gets them all mixed up with hilarious results.

The search for a fourth young noble began. More than ten actors who were regular participants in the programmes run by the Foundation came for auditions. They did improvisations with the other actors, but Corinne could not see what she was looking for in any of them. Like most Afghans, they confused acting with overacting. She worked with each of them to see if she could help them tone down their performances, but without success.

By then, Ariane Mnouchkine was in Kabul conducting workshops at the Foundation. With a nod to her Paris-based Theatre du Soleil, she was setting up a training programme for actors that she called 'Groupe Aftab.' 'Aftab' is the Dari word for sun, much as 'soleil' is in French. Many members of the Groupe Aftab were students at Kabul

University's Faculty of Fine Arts. One of them was a young actor named Arif Bahonar.

Arif had that spark that every director looks for. A handsome young Hazara, he had a sense of freshness about him. He understood subtlety. Perhaps that had come from his work with Ariane, or perhaps it was something innate. Regardless, from the first day he came, Corinne wanted him for our production.

With Arif on board, we had four solid actors lined up for the young nobles, even though Corinne was still trying to decide who would play which character. That meant that *Love's Labour's Lost* was now halfway to being possible.

∾

Before she began looking for actresses, however, Corinne held a session with the actors to talk about the plays that Shakespeare had written and to get their reactions to them. As we all sat on *toshaks*, floor cushions, in the grand salon, she started by explaining that Shakespeare had written tragedies and comedies, and we could think about doing any of them. The actors quickly made it clear that they wanted nothing to do with tragedy.

Nabi Tanha said, "We have lived tragedy for three decades of war. We want to do comedy."

Shah Mohammed agreed. "A tragedy play is too soon now," he added. "Let's make people laugh. When the time comes, we will do a tragedy, and we will take our revenge. Revenge is like a thirst, but a thirst that cannot be quenched with water. The thirst of revenge can only be quenched by seeing the blood of enemies. We will show some blood on the stage to quench the great thirst of families of victims." Corinne, who is exceptionally articulate, was momentarily at a loss for words.

Arif spoke very forcefully, adding, "When we do a tragedy, we will write our own play, and not use Shakespeare's. Our tragedy will be far more intense than any tragedy he ever made. We will write it the way it happened: the planes came, circled high in the distance above us, then dropped bombs on our houses, our schools, our hospitals, and made them blast open as one collapsed after another, or sometimes several of them at the same time. Windows and doors blew out, and flames rose in giant mushroom-shaped smoke mixed with dust, and the air smelled of gunpowder, with women and children shouting out in fear or for help. The whole ground shook, and it felt like an earthquake. That is our tragedy, and we will write it."

Nabi Tanha had become fired up while he listened to Arif's story. "When the Russians withdrew," Nabi Tanha said, "there then came the seven idiots from Pakistan." We all knew he meant the seven factions. "And civil war started." Then he looked at Shah Mohammed, and shouted with blood lust, "I'm gonna kill you, because you're a Pashtun."

Shah Mohammed sprang to his feet as he rasped, "No, I'm gonna kill you, because you are a Hazara." They were improvising, but they had instantly sent a chill through the room until Faisal shouted, "I'm gonna kill you both, because neither of you are Uzbek." Everyone laughed. It was the first of many times that a well-timed joke by Faisal would defuse a situation headed towards overheating.

Arif said, "And then came the black period, the Taliban, with their dirty *shalwar kamiz*, their long black and white turbans, their mouths full of snuff, their eyes outlined by *kohl*, and ugly weapons hanging from their shoulders."

Nabi Tanha shouted in a coarse voice in Pashto, "School is banned for women. Nor are they allowed to work outside of the house, and they should cover their heads when they go out."

Shah Mohammed, in an even harsher voice, continued, "All men should grow beards and be present in the mosque five times a day for prayers."

"No one can keep pigeons or any fighting birds or animals in the house," Faisal added in a deep Kandahari-accented Pashto, "We will monitor everything, and if we find anyone with fighting birds or animals, we will punish them."

He looked at everyone like a Taliban, with fierce eyes, until he suddenly exploded in laughter. And we all laughed. Then, he made fierce eyes again, and we all stopped laughing. He said, "No kite flying for kids or anyone else." Again, he burst out laughing, and we all did, too. He was revealing a power as an actor that we had not seen yet.

Everybody had a story to tell as they recounted the history of the past three decades in Afghanistan, from the invasion of the Russians to the arrival of the Americans.

Corinne listened to them thoughtfully, and asked many questions. As she did, the actors realised that there were large gaps in her knowledge of Afghanistan's peoples, history, cultures and customs. They saw that their time with Corinne would be a two-way conversation. She would teach them about theatre and Shakespeare; they would teach her about Afghanistan.

∾

Every day, Corinne and I were learning new things about the actors. We would all sit on floor cushions in the old salon, and talk at length. The conversations were quiet and thoughtful. One day we were talking about acting and why the *bachaha*, "the boys," as Corinne was now calling them, had become interested in acting.

Faisal smiled, and said, "Acting is an art, like painting, wood carving or calligraphy. None of these arts are easy when you first start, but once you are in the sea of it, you will swim for the rest of your life, even though you know that you can never reach your destination.

"I became addicted to acting at school when everybody clapped for me after I performed the role of a lazy student on Teacher's Day. I was ten or twelve years old. I was immediately addicted to it like some people are to opium, or a bee is to honey. But I didn't learn it in an academic way. I have never been to an acting class all my life. When you have the hunger for something, and you do not have a school; your talent becomes your school."

Nabi Tanha, by contrast, had studied acting at Kabul University's Faculty of Fine Arts. He told us, "I'm not just an actor, I also write screenplays, I direct movies, I montage and edit movies, I act in both movies and theatre, and I'm a good cameraman, too. You should come to my studio sometime, or you should watch my film *Bulbul*, which is very famous. And I am very famous, too. When I go out, people call me Bulbul, as if my real name is Bulbul," which means nightingale.

As the production evolved, we learned that Nabi Tanha was a good *tabla* player, as well as an expert on the harmonium and the flute.

Whenever Shah Mohammed is about to speak, he rocks forward

and back a couple of times, the way some people clear their throat. When Nabi Tanha had finished speaking, Shah Mohammed rocked forward twice.

"Everything I know about acting," Shah Mohammed then said, "I learned from my good friend and teacher, Nabi Tanha. I didn't learn acting in an academic way. I learned it from Nabi jan, by doing it."

When Nabi Tanha directs a movie, Shah Mohammed is his assistant. When Nabi writes a screenplay, Shah Mohammed is his assistant. When Nabi is a cameraman for a movie, Shah Mohammed is his assistant. Nabi Tanha and Shah Mohammed get into loud fights all the time, but five minutes later they laugh at whatever had come between them.

Shah Mohammed had worked for eighteen years in Afghanistan television as an announcer. Now with Nabi Tanha, he was making commercials for Afghanistan's fast-growing number of television networks. "After the Taliban collapsed," he told us, "I stepped into the world of movies, and discovered what it means to be an actor." As the months passed, we saw that he took acting very seriously and was a complete professional in the way he dealt with everyone else.

Kabir Rahimi was the oldest among the actors. He always sat in a corner, and did not say much. He did mention, though, that he also had studied acting at Kabul University. Kabir was always ready with a smile, but said very little about himself. "I directed a few movies and theatre plays, and I am a playwright for both movie and theatre," he mentioned one day. "I can easily get the picture of a situation, and put it into a play, and make it funny."

Afghans rarely talk about their personal or family lives to strangers. And when Corinne asked questions about them, the actors were polite, but vague. Over time, though, as we began to get to know each other, the individuals behind the actors' masks came a little bit into focus.

Nabi Tanha was married with several children, including a set of twins. He has the North Asian features of his Mongolian ancestors, whose descendants came to Afghanistan in numerous waves denoted as Turkmen, Hazara, Uzbek, Qizilbash and others. Some from each group look almost Chinese; others appear quite different owing to extensive intermarriage over the centuries with women taken from other groups. Afghans are ethnically very mixed, but usually identify only with their fathers' people.

Shah Mohammed is a Tajik. He and his wife are the only ones of all their relatives who live in Afghanistan. All the rest are in Europe, Canada, or America. Shah Mohammed has had chances to leave, but has turned them down. "Perhaps I am mad," he says, "but I love Afghanistan."

His wife is a teacher at a girls school. They have six children and want them to live in an Islamic society, especially their five daughters. He does not want them to grow up with the values of the young people he sees in the western media. All of his children are getting good education. His goal, he said, is for each one of his daughters to have a university degree before he gives permission for them to marry.

Arif grew up in a poor family. No one in his family had ever been an actor. He had a wife who, like himself, is a Hazara. She lived with his parents in Ghazni province, about two hours south of Kabul on the road to Kandahar. Their marriage had been arranged by their fathers. They had no children yet, but one day he boasted playfully that, "In a few years there will be a team of football players in my house, and I will be the trainer."

As a student in the Fine Arts Faculty of the Theatre Department at the Kabul University, he had very few chances to visit his wife who lived with his parents. He could go home, he said, only about once a month for a day or two.

In Kabul, Arif lived in the large dormitory at the university where the food was poor, water unpredictable, electricity rare, and several students crowded into one room. No one complained, though, as their goal was not to be comfortable, but to learn. At night when there was no electricity and they needed to study, they would sit in clumps under the streetlamps, reading.

❧

One day, Corinne asked the actors to talk about their experiences in the war years, but they did not want to.

Shah Mohammed said, "Why should I give you a headache with my sad stories? Our history in my lifetime is nothing but war. Why should I bore you with that?"

Nabi Tanha sighed, "People are so stupid fighting for a king or a president whom they never will see. There would have been fewer wars if the leaders had to fight each other, rather than send young men into bloodthirsty battle fields."

Faisal added, "The men who are the most powerful are the most foolish, while lesser men are really wiser and good men."

"Like me?" Nabi Tanha said.

"Like all of us," Kabir said, with a sad smile.

Arif was quiet all this time. He sighed deeply, "I'm a man of sense, or at least try to be. I don't let myself be disturbed by the ups and downs of life; I learned this from my father. I may be rich or poor, but neither matters to me. What is important to me is always having respect for other human beings, for nature and trying not to injure them, or their feelings. I always try my best to forgive them if they injure me.

"My conscience is more important to me than my anger for revenge from those who injured me physically or psychologically during those years of war," he said. "I have no fear of death, for it is a natural thing, even if it doesn't always happen naturally."

Everyone was quiet for a few moments. Then Faisal started telling a story that we would hear many times again as our weeks together passed. Whenever he told it, he always had a big smile as if he were being reminded of an old joke that was still very funny to him.

One day a couple of years before, he told us, he was hanging out with five of his closest friends in front of their houses, not far from the front door of the Foundation. All of them had grown up in that neighbourhood, and had known each other since they were little kids flying homemade kites from the rooftops. Without warning a rocket hit the ground a few steps from where they were standing. It exploded, and all five of his friends were killed instantly.

"I am the only one who survived," he would say with his eyes gleeful. Then he would show a mass of scars on his legs, arm, and back. "This is my gift from Hekmatyar," referring to the leader of one of the factions, Gulbuddin Hekmatyar.

At the end Faisal would always say, "You know, God saved me! By now I should have been turned into dust, but God saved me, and here I am doing Shakespeare." Then he would laugh.

7

Casting: The Girls

Kabul. May, 2005.

The time had come to start auditioning actresses. Corinne asked the actors to invite any women they knew who would be interested. Robert Kluijver also sent out word to the universities and elsewhere.

On the day of the first audition, a group of women were waiting for us at the Foundation when we arrived. Some were young, some middle-aged, some old. It was a hot day. The weather had turned unseasonably warm as an early heat wave swept over Kabul, chasing away the mountain air that is usually still cool in May.

The women were sitting on chairs arranged in small groups on the grass, chatting with each other. When they saw us come into the garden, they stood up very formally, and greeted us.

Corinne introduced herself, and described the nature of the project. She told them that she needed five good and talented actresses. We soon found out, though, that many of them had never appeared either on stage or in front of a camera. Several were housewives who just wanted to do something different. With the Taliban gone, they had thrown open the cage of the *burqa*, and were ready to fly. They had decided to become actresses, to express their hopes and sorrows through acting.

When Corinne asked them to do an improvisation as an audition, they all looked puzzled. None of them knew what an improvisation was. None, except for a girl named Leila.

Leila had come with her mother. Her father was an actor who appeared regularly on Afghan television. She asked if she could play the role of an angry mother, who is buried under too much housework. Corinne told her to go ahead.

Leila stood up, rolled up her sleeves, and pretended that she was slicing onions. She kept wiping the tears coming out of her eyes with the back of her hand, while she was shouting at her kids to get out of the kitchen. Then one of them knocks all her spices onto the kitchen floor. As she is gathering them up, a pot she had on the stove catches fire. The kids start crying as her husband comes in and shouts at her. She shouts back at her husband to help her pour water on the fire, but instead he comes and beats her with a ladle, a pot and a plate. All the time the children keep crying, and everything is a complete mess.

Corinne whispered to me, "She is good for a girl who has never done acting before." I nodded.

Leila finished. Corinne clapped, and everybody else clapped as well. Corinne looked at Leila's mother and said, "Your daughter is very good." An appreciative smile appeared on Leila's mother's face. Jokingly, Corinne asked, "Was she pretending to be you?"

Leila's mother's face turned bright red. Abruptly she said, "No." After a few seconds of thought, however, she smiled and said, "Maybe." Corinne asked Leila about herself.

Leila replied that she was in the seventh grade, though she was eighteen. Like many young Afghans, she had had few opportunities for formal schooling during the war years, because either they were living in refugee camps in other countries where schools did not exist, or they had remained in the Taliban's Afghanistan, where girls were forbidden to study. Leila and her family had fled to Iran. She spoke Dari with a strong Farsi accent. Sometimes I could not understand her, and had to ask her to repeat what she had said several times.

Now all the other women knew what improvisation meant. They wanted to do their own. They started moving their chairs back to create a space in which to perform. One woman whose face was very familiar to me stood up. Several of the other women nodded to each other when she did, as if they had recognised her as well. I was not sure why I felt I knew her.

She was in her late thirties, and had a way about her that suggested she was accustomed to being in charge. She started to explain what she wanted to do, but Corinne stopped her, and told her just to show it in acting. She said, "Okay," and lay down on the floor with on one elbow resting on a pillow. She called her daughter, as she was fingering an imaginary beard. We quickly understood that she was impersonating a man. In a deep, rough voice, the man demanded a glass of green tea, which he then took from the girl.

The man took one sip, and spat it out. He looked at his imaginary daughter and shouted angrily, "Is this tea, or donkey's piss? Why is it cold? Why is the cardamom missing? You daughter of a whore! Do you know why I killed your mother? Because she was disrespectful! Get me some good tea, daughter of a bitch!" Then the man turned his head away, but kept shouting after her.

"When you have done that, tidy the house. There are some suitors coming today. One of them is the Khan of the upper town. He is asking for your hand. I said 'Yes' to him in the field yesterday. He is coming with his family to make it official." Then the man looked up at the daughter, and asked harshly, "Why are you crying? What? Say again! You are too young to be married? Who says so?! I know you learned these things from your whore mother. I should have killed her long before I did."

The man changed his tone to what he probably thought was reasonable. "You are sixteen. Sixteen is marriageable. What? What did you say? Speak louder! The Khan is older than you? So what? He is my age. Are you telling me that I'm too old, and I can't marry a sixteen year old? Shut up, daughter of a bitch! You can't find better than the Khan. He is the leader of his tribe. What did you say? He has two more wives? So what? He is allowed to marry four wives. Who are you to say what you will do? I'm your father, and I will decide. Stop crying, or I'll crush you under my feet." The man continued fingering his imaginary beard.

Suddenly, the man became an actress again, and she burst out laughing. She looked at Corinne, and asked in English, "Good?"

"Very good!" Corinne said, "And look, you speak English."

"A little," she said with a hint of shyness that had not been evident in her improvisation.

"You are a good actor," Corinne said.

"Thank you," she said in English.

"What is your name?"

"Breshna Bahar," she said.

Now I knew where I had seen her. Throughout her improvisation, I had been trying to remember.

"Where did you learn acting?" Corinne asked.

She didn't understand the question, so I had to repeat it in Dari.

"I've been doing acting for several years. I'm known for my part in the *Bulbul* movie with Nabi Tanha. I am Gul Chaira. When people on the street see me, they call me Gul Chaira." She went on to say, "I'm also a policewoman, and I have done plays and movies. If you want, I can get you some copies."

"Oh, I would love to see them," Corinne replied enthusiastically. Then she looked at me and said softly, "She is wild, isn't she?" I nodded.

"Okay, Breshna jan. I'll talk to you later," Corinne told her. I chuckled, because Corinne had already picked up the Afghan habit of adding "jan" to somebody's name. It is a sign of affection and respect. And Afghans say it to almost everyone, whether or not they actually have any affection or respect for them.

Afterwards, Corinne said she was worried that Breshna Bahar was too hard-edged to play a noble lady. She kept Breshna Bahar's contact information, but was not sure about having her in the show, though she had enjoyed the improvisation. Later, as we were leaving the Foundation, we saw Breshna Bahar driving her own car. That is very rare for a woman in Afghanistan.

"Interesting," nodded Corinne as she and Breshna Bahar waved to each other. Later in our car she added, "She is someone I would like to get to know."

Breshna Bahar might be "wild," but I guessed then that she would be in the cast, and it turned out that I was right.

∽

Then next day, as we arrived at the Foundation, a new group of women were waiting for us. We did improvisations with all of them, more than ten in all. None were as good as Breshna Bahar or Leila. We gathered their phone numbers, and said goodbyes.

We were about to leave the Foundation for home when Parwin Mushtahel arrived. She apologised for being late, explaining that she had been stuck in one of the terrible traffic jams that clog Kabul's streets several times a day.

Corinne explained that we were about to leave, and would see her the next day, but Parwin insisted. It was difficult for her to come the great distance from her home to the Foundation, and she wanted to do the audition and be done with it. In the end, Corinne agreed.

Parwin told us, "I would like to do an improvisation about a widowed woman who lost her husband and son in the civil war, and now she is going to commit suicide, but she is laughing and very happy, though she is not insane. But before she hangs herself, she wants the world to know what she went through, and why she is ending her life."

Corinne looked hesitant, and said, "I think that's a little too grim."

"It is based on real life," Parwin said, "In fact, the woman was our neighbour."

"Okay, let's do it," Corinne said. She looked a little tired, because of the hot weather, and sat down on a cushion. Corinne had sat in chairs the first few times she had come for auditions. Now she was becoming an Afghan, and making herself comfortable sitting on the floor on the long, flat *toshaks*, and leaning against the wall.

Parwin stood in the middle of the room on a chair. Her face turned serious, and she began.

"Life has no meaning for me anymore. Life lost its meaning on the day that a blind rocket from Gulbuddin landed on our roof, and took my son away from me forever. He was only eight years old, but so handsome. Large dark brown eyes, a little nose, curly black hair, smooth and spotless skin.

"I bathed him, played with him, splashed water on him, played hide and seek with him, made sand palaces with him, drew animals with him, and flew kites with him. He couldn't pronounce the letter 'S'. Only 'Sh'.

"My Omar used to tell me strange and funny stories, all the work of his imagination. He used to start this way: 'There was a jungle that had many animals. They were all friends with each other. They had kings. All the kings had wings. God made them kings from their birth.'

"I asked him, 'What about snakes or elephants?'"

"He said, 'Their kings had wings, too.'"

"I asked him, 'What about the birds? They all have wings already. Were they all kings?'"

"He thought for a second and said, 'There are no birds in that forest.'"

I could feel Omar present in the room with us. Parwin had made him real. She went on.

"Life in those days was nothing but a chain of struggles, of fear and of death. But you, Omar jan, made my black days as bright as the sun. And one day while I was in the kitchen cooking for you, your favourite dessert, *ferni*, a blind rocket from Gulbuddin landed on your room while you were still asleep, and you still had not told me your dreams from that night.

"The noise of the rocket was so loud that I could not hear anything. I was dizzy, and everything smelled of gunpowder, and dust was everywhere as if it had conquered the whole earth. I staggered to your room, and saw a big mound of rubble, all in a pile, the roof beams, the mud bricks. But there was no trace of you. Several times I shouted, 'Omar jan, where are you?', but I didn't hear your sweet voice. I continued shouting.

"My shouts were echoing inside my own skull, a hundred times louder than ever before. I shouted so much that I lost my voice. I noticed the neighbours had come into the courtyard, all the men, standing around me, watching me, but none of them dared to come close to me. I was like a madwoman, shouting, slapping myself, crying, pulling my hair, and tearing my clothes, but no one calmed me.

"Your father Karim came home. He had only just gone out to get some fresh bread for breakfast. When he saw me in such a state, he covered me with his *patu*, but I kept shouting and crying. He covered me with his arms, and kissed me on my head as he repeatedly said, 'Calm down, calm down.' But how could I calm down? I had just lost my sweetheart, my Omar. I had lost my calmness forever. I will not ever feel like a human again. I was something else now. I continued shouting as I lost consciousness."

As Parwin stood on the chair, she was creating a whole universe centred on this woman's pain and despair.

"When I woke up, I found myself in my bed alone, and the sun was pouring into the room. I didn't know why I was sleeping at such an hour of the day. It was almost midday. I had a terrible headache. I went to the mirror to tidy myself before going out, but I saw something in the mirror that scared me to my core. It was the face of a woman with disheveled hair, a scratched face, eyes red like fireballs, and torn clothes. 'Who is this woman?' I asked myself. 'Is this me? What happened to me?'

"Suddenly, the mirror shattered into bits, and I could no longer see myself. The air was filled with the smell of gunpowder mixed with dust. I ran out of the room to find out what had happened. All I could see was a cloud of dust rising to the sky. I knew right away that another of Gulbuddin's blind rockets had landed on the same room where you, my son, had been buried under all that rubble. And this time, this rocket had killed my husband who had been trying to dig your body from under the pile of dirt.

"My eyes were dry. There was not a single tear left to come out. So instead, I laughed. I laughed: Ha ha ha ha ha ha ha…. Soon all the neighbours came again, and saw me laughing. This time, their women came too. They thought I had lost my mind, but they didn't know I was crying with my laughter.

"I noticed the women weeping for me, and I felt jealous towards them that they had tears to shed for me, yet I had no tears to shed for my husband and my sweetheart little boy. I laughed, ha ha ha ha ha ha….."

Parwin filled the room with a chilling laugh that sent shivers down my spine. Her eyes grew wide now, as she picked up something in front of her.

"I found a sharp piece of metal. It was a fragment of the blind rocket. It was sharp like a butcher's knife. I lifted it up to stab into my stomach, but I was grabbed by a man who gripped my wrists. I struggled, but couldn't succeed. I lost consciousness again, and collapsed.

"When I woke up, I saw my sister looking at me. She kissed me, and told me that I had been sleeping for four days. 'For so long?' I asked myself.

"Suddenly, I remembered everything. I cried. This time, really crying. Not laughing. I didn't just cry for my husband and son, I cried for not having been there to cry on the day when their coffins had been taken out of the house. I cried for what I saw. I cried for my future. I cried that I will never be able to smile again. I cried for all those mothers and widows who have lost their dear ones. I cried for my country. I cried for everything that is wrong in our lives."

Tears were streaming down Parwin's cheeks. And mine.

"My eyes were like springs, and tears continued falling, wetting my face, burning my cheeks. Everything looked blurry, and tears still kept coming. From that day, I never stopped. I know that my heart will keep crying until the moment of death. I don't know when death will claim me. Maybe not for a very long time. So today I'm going to claim death.

"I want to stop this crying. My dear ones are in paradise. I want to see them. And today I shall. The journey is short. This rope in my hands is my transportation."

Parwin held up an imaginary rope as a frightening kind of joy filled her face.

"One end of this rope is tied to the ceiling. This end is in my hands. I will put it around my neck, and then I will push the chair from under my feet. I know it is going to be painful. But pain has no meaning for me anymore. Physical pain is nothing compared to the pain in my heart and my soul.

"Let me take a last good look at this room. The floor is covered with carpets that Karim and I bought. I remember buying that TV with him, and that videocassette player. The first film we watched was our wedding film. I remember that cradle in the corner of the room. Omar jan grew up in that cradle. He would have been fifteen years old by now, as handsome as his father. Seven years have passed without him. Seven years! All these years, I cried even in my dreams. Now it is time for laughing.

"I have to laugh. I have to go, and laugh with my Omar jan and my Karim jan. We will laugh together. Oh my God! I'm smiling now. After seven years, I'm smiling. A smile is a promise of laughter.

"Goodbye, cries. Laughter, wait for me. I'm coming towards you. I'm very close. Here, I'm coming."

Then she pushed the chair from under her feet.

Corinne looked at me. Her eyes had welled up with tears, though she had not understood a word of what Parwin had said. But the tragic energy generated by Parwin had transferred to Corinne as strongly as it had to me. While we fought back tears, Parwin stood in front of us with a big smile on her face.

Corinne and I clapped, but I could not stop my tears from falling. I had not cried for years. Parwin had just narrated my childhood, from the time I turned eight, and the Mujahedin had started their cruel and pointless war. Not even the Russians, whom we had hated and defeated, had treated us as badly as the factional commanders of the Mujahedin.

For fifteen years, day after day, year after year, I had lived through what Parwin had just described. Now, how could I stop my tears from falling? I had not cried even once in those fifteen years. I knew that I must be brave now, swallow my sorrows, and shut my eyes against my tears, and keep them there. I knew I could not defeat them once they took control of me.

Now, suddenly, Parwin started to cry, as if all my tears had found a new home in her eyes. Corinne hugged her, and started rubbing her back, but I could still hear her sobs as she shook in Corinne's arms.

I had to walk away. I could not stand being there for another minute. I made a slow circle around the garden. How many nights had we sat in our house as bombs fell around us? How many days had we known that this was our last day on earth? How many screams had we heard when our neighbours had been hit, or had been knocked deaf by the blast that killed all sound when it exploded too close?

I sat at the far end of the garden for several minutes until I could push all these unwanted memories back into the deep hole of the past where I tried so hard to keep them. By the time I returned to the room, Parwin was smiling, though her eyes were still glistening. She apologised to me for stirring up my emotions. I simply said, "*Mushkel n'ast*." Dari for "No problem."

Corinne looked at me, and asked me if I was okay. I smiled, and said, "Yes," though I was still crying in my heart of hearts for that woman, who only God knows if she is still alive or is with her husband and her son.

Corinne asked me to please interpret. As my voice was shaking, I told Parwin what Corinne just said: "Parwin jan, Corinne says you are a good actress. Though our play is not about tragedy, you are good, and she would like you to be part of it."

A shy smile appeared on Parwin's face as she hugged Corinne.

"Was she a close friend?" Corinne asked. "Your neighbour?"

Parwin shrugged. "We knew each other," she said. "Her brother and sisters moved away a few weeks later. I never saw any of them again. That is how it is here in Afghanistan. We never know how things end." A few minutes later, she left.

～

The next day, none of the women who came to audition had had any previous experience. They tried hard, but were not ready to perform. Among them was a woman who looked to be about eighty years old. She was hardly one meter tall. Corinne was polite and told her, "I don't think I would have a part for you in this play. Maybe for the next one." But we kept her phone number, because we were getting worried that we might not find anyone else.

A day later, I spotted a tall woman with a lot of make-up among those who had come to audition. Her eyelashes were covered with heavy mascara, and her eyebrows had high arches blackened by eyebrow pencil. As I shook hands with her, I remembered that she was Sabah Sahar, a well-known actress who had appeared in many Afghan movies. Frequently, she played the role of a policewoman.

I spoke to her with the enthusiasm of a fan, gushing, "It is a great pleasure meeting you! I have seen several of your movies, and I liked them all."

"Thank you very much!" she said graciously, smiling.

I had also read in the local newspapers that she had travelled to Europe and several Asian countries to talk about her movies, or to raise funds to make new ones. She owned and ran a film production company, Sabah Film. I had not been expecting to see her at the auditions, because I assumed that she would not work for the low wages we would be paying. But before I could get to that, she spoke as if she had been reading my mind.

"I have heard some interesting things about Corinne, and I was told by the Foundation that she is going to do Shakespeare. I love

Shakespeare. I used to do Shakespeare at University. I love his irony, his unpredictability, yet his writing is so clear and poetic. It is not something that we often have had a chance to do. I would like to do it."

Good, I thought, she is not here for the money, but for Shakespeare.

Corinne looked at me smiling, but slightly annoyed, and asked me jokingly, "Are you still working for me?" which meant I had been enjoying my chat with Sabah Sahar so much that I had forgotten to interpret what she had just said for Corinne. So, I did.

Corinne asked Sabah Sahar if she could do some improvisations. Sabah Sahar gave a look that suggested that she felt she was too well established in her profession to be asked to improvise.

Corinne turned to me with a look that asked, "What is with her? Does she think she is too good for us?" I shrugged my shoulders, not wanting to get caught between two strong personalities.

Sabah Sahar asked whom she was supposed to play.

Corinne said, "Anything that you are comfortable with." Then she changed her mind, suggesting, "Why not play a policewoman, since you have done that in many of your movies?"

"I would rather do something royal, if you don't mind, a princess for instance," Sabah Sahar responded.

"Go ahead," Corinne said.

Sabah Sahar stood and walked to the centre of the room. When she turned to face us again, she had become a different person. "I'm going to play a Persian princess whose fiancé is from Iraq," she said as she looked around at everyone in the room. "He has left her for another woman, whom everybody thinks of as a prostitute. This story sounds like a Shakespeare play. Shakespeare is all about love, betrayals, lies, killings, disappearances, mysteries, sadism, absurdisms, because these topics don't get old. After all, all our lives encompass these things."

"You seem to know a lot about Shakespeare," Corinne interrupted.

"He is one of my favourite playwrights," Sabah Sahar said, and launched into her improvisation with a cold whisper.

"I don't understand him. How come he betrayed me? Every angle I consider turns into a puzzle for me. How, after so much love and patience, after so many declarations, vows, sighs, tears, passions, passionate letters, ardent protestations, and repeated promises could he have betrayed me – not just me, but my family, my country, his family, and his country? What does that whore have that I don't have? What happened to all those promises?"

She was good. She had already snared my attention and was stirring my imagination. Most of the other women who had auditioned previously had rooted themselves in one place. But Sabah Sahar was moving all over the room, as if she were in a house where she had lived all her life. She made us feel like intruders.

"I was not in love with him, and I still am not. But I was falling in love with him, and he was growing in me. I had dreamed that by marrying him I would bury myself in passion forever. He used to tell me I was beautiful. He used to tell me, 'Your beauty delights me whenever I look at you.' He used to tell me, 'I want to give over to the sweet violence of love, and let you rule me. I had thousands of hearts offered to me, but when I saw you, I gave them all up. Now I only love you, and have you alone in my heart.' Was he lying? Why?

"Are all men liars? No, not Rumi. He was in love all his life, but his love was for God, while mine was for God's creation. Maybe love is not true unless it is for God. No! Love is madness. Love is stupidity. Love is betrayal. Or maybe love is only a mere and empty word, but we give it all kinds of meanings.

"I wish I had stayed a child forever when everybody used to say to me, 'I love you,' and they were kind. When I was little, 'love' meant tenderness. As I grew older, the meaning has changed. Now I'm not sure what it is. I believe in God, but I don't believe in love now. I don't believe in many things now. Man is one of them.

"No! Many men are decent. Our prophets were men. They told us of truth. They led us to the right path, the path of God. Men are not all bad. Only this one."

Sabah Sahar's voice was now low and cool, but it was filled with the fire of scorn.

"Ah, a breaker is always a breaker. He broke my heart, and he will break hers, whomever he is with now. And his betrayals towards so many will turn into a fierce enemy one day, and will lead to his end. As for me, I must restore my belief in men. I need time for that. Time and patience; they are key to unlocking the miseries and opening doors to happiness. Time and patience."

She stopped, and remained motionless for several moments. We did as well. I had had difficulty translating what she said, because she used a high form of Dari that we usually find only in literature. Her speaking was almost like poetry. The best I could do was to interpret the gist of it. But my mind was ablaze with the excitement of hearing her throw poetic couplets into the air like rose petals.

Corinne seemed to have understood that, even without my interpreting Sabah Sahar's monologue for her precisely. I was learning that language does not have to be a barrier between theatre artists. They can comprehend each other in other ways.

"You are very good," Corinne said to Sabah Sahar.

Sabah Sahar acknowledged the compliment with a slight nod. Corinne told Sabah Sahar that she would like to have her in the cast. Sabah Sahar asked Corinne to let her know a week in advance before the start of the project, because she had many projects of her own. In the Afghan way, she asked permission to leave, then walked gracefully out of the room.

"She's good," Corinne said to me as she left. "But she's going to have to get rid of all that make-up if she's going to be in this show."

All the other women who had come to audition that day felt small with Sabah Sahar there. They all knew they could not perform as well as she. Two of them quietly walked out of the room soon after she did, and never came back.

We continued auditioning for a couple of more days, and, though we saw many women, none had the skills needed.

∾

Corinne had been talking about Marina Gulbahari since she had come back from Paris. Marina had broken hearts around the world when she had played the title role in the film *Osama*. She was probably the best known actress in Afghanistan. But where was she? Corinne asked Robert if he could help us find her. He said he would try. But even he did not know where to look for her.

8

Casting: Searching for Marina

Kabul. June, 2005.

I had read about Marina Gulbahari when *Osama* came out in 2003. Though she had been a beggar only a few years before, Marina had become the face of Afghanistan's new film industry. *Osama* had brought the Afghan cinema to the Cannes Film Festival for the first time in history, and it won awards both there and in London.

A few months later when *Osama* made its way to the Kabul pirate CD market, I had a chance to watch it. Marina played the role of a young girl who tries to survive the madness of the Taliban by pretending to be a boy, so she can earn money for her family. I could not take my eyes off her. Her face was like an encyclopedia of human emotion, as one after another swept across it.

I knew very little about Marina. My sources of information were several local newspapers and magazines that had interviewed her about her life and *Osama*. Her family had sunk into desperate poverty. She was forced to endure the humiliation of begging in the streets. She begged for scraps from the tables of Kabul restaurants, where she would get a few crumpled notes or *kebab* leftovers wrapped in *naan*, the unleavened bread that Afghans eat with every meal.

When I saw an interview on TV with Siddiq Barmak, the director of *Osama*, I felt proud that we had such educated Afghans who were raising the flag of Afghanistan in France and England after so many years of war and devastation. Barmak said that he chairs the Afghan Children's Education Movement, an association founded by Iranian film director Mohsen Makhmalbaf and originally based in Iran to help Afghan refugees there. The school trained young Afghans in acting and directing.

I had read in a newspaper how Siddiq Barmak had found Marina. She came to beg for food from the table in a restaurant where he was eating. At the time, he was looking for a young girl to cast as Osama. He was struck by the beggar girl's charisma. She had a certain something that he had not seen in any of the other girls he had auditioned. He did a few shots of her with a small video camera, and was amazed at the way her personality filled the screen. He asked her to take him to meet her father. Before long, Marina would go from begging to becoming Afghanistan's most famous cinema celebrity. She was about ten years old at the time, but like many Afghans was unsure of her age.

Fame in Afghanistan, though, does not come with a fixed address. We did not know where to find her. We were told that she still lived in a refugee camp near Kabul Stadium. Robert talked to everyone he knew, but could find no contacts for her.

We presumed that Siddiq Barmak knew where she was, but at the time, he was out of the country. One day when I had an emergency at home and could not accompany her, Corinne went to the refugee camp by herself. It had been a small city of tents for many years. When she got there, though, she found that only a few tents were left. The United Nations, which had been running the camp, was in the process of shutting it down. Its residents were being moved into permanent shelter.

Marina's family was not there, and none of the refugees knew where she lived. In fact, they had never heard of her.

After a few weeks, Barmak returned to Kabul, and Robert learned from him that Marina's family was living in a poor neighbourhood known as Char Qala-e-Wazir Abad.

∽

Her house was on a small backstreet with a narrow drainage ditch running down the middle filled with the human waste from the toilets of the houses on both sides. Kabul has no sewers, despite all the aid that foreign governments say they have given us. The stink from the ditch burned our noses. Thousands of flies that had been dancing in it flew up in our faces in large swarms, displeased at having been disturbed. Their buzzing was loud enough to be frightening.

I knocked on a metal door that we guessed was Marina's. We heard dogs barking. A minute later, a little girl opened the door a crack. I told her that we were there to see her sister, Marina.

The girl shouted, "Marina, Marina, Marina, here are some people who want to see you." Then she looked up at us and smiled sweetly. As she opened the door a bit wider, I noticed that she was barefoot.

Marina ran towards the door, also barefoot. Before she even said hello she giggled. She opened the door wide for us to walk in. Then she said, "Salaam, please come in. *Kaka* (uncle) Barmak told me about you."

We walked into the little courtyard. There were two massive dogs chained to a stake in the ground, barking nonstop. Next to a well were some unwashed dishes from the dinner the night before, which Marina said she had been washing, but she had heard an Indian song on TV that she liked, and left the dishes for later.

Marina led us to a small room with *toshak* cushions arranged along the walls. A TV in the corner was still showing the Indian song. A Bollywood actress named Kajol was singing and dancing with Shah Rukh Khan.

Corinne said, "I tried to find you at the refugee camp near the Stadium."

Marina giggled again. "We moved from there a long time ago. My film career enabled me to buy this small house," she said.

She asked for my name and Corinne's, and I told her. I also told her a little about our project. She said that she would love to work with Corinne to learn new things about acting. She told us that she had never done theatre before. She was not sure what theatre was. I tried to explain.

She asked me, "Is it without cutting and stopping?" Corinne told her "You have to be on stage for two hours, and cannot miss a word." She was surprised, and said, "Oh, that is impossible!"

Corinne asked her if she was still going to school, and she said that she had reached the fourth grade. She said that she thought she was fifteen. Or maybe sixteen. She was not sure.

Suddenly, a warning bell rang in my mind, and I asked myself, "How will she be able to perform Shakespeare if she is only in the fourth grade? Each word of Shakespeare has more than one meaning, and acting depends on knowing them." But I told myself that this was a problem for the future.

She said that she had been discouraged from going to school by some people whose names she did not want to say. "They tell me that 'You don't need to go to school. You are a famous actress now.'" The headmaster at her school told her, "You have to decide on one, either school or the movies." So, she stopped going to school.

A few minutes later, she brought us green tea in a very nice Chinese pot with cups on their saucers arranged on an ornate silver tray. As she poured us tea, the smell of cardamom reached my nose. For her work on *Osama*, she told us that she was paid $6,000.00. Some of that money had been used to buy beautiful things for her family's new house.

Corinne asked her question after question about her life, family, film career, Siddiq Barmak, and life in Afghanistan.

She giggled more than she talked, and was very pleasant and cheerful. We found out that she was one of ten brothers and sisters, and all from one mother. Two of her sisters were married and lived separately with their husbands, one in Iran and another in Kabul. She had lost two of her older sisters in the civil war. The rest were living in that little courtyard with their parents.

Her father used to sell Bollywood audio cassettes, but now he was jobless, and spent most of his time with his dogs, fighting them, betting on them, and winning or losing money. Her brothers were still in school, as well as her sisters. Her mother was a housewife.

After *Osama*, she had appeared in some other Afghan movies. They had not achieved the fame of *Osama*, but I had seen them, and thought that they were as good as *Osama*, and perhaps even better in some ways.

She told us, "I have been in some Asian countries for film festivals. I was given a gold horse medal at one of them, but it was stolen before it actually got to me." She giggled. "But I was told that it was just covered in gold, and it did not cost that much, so not to worry about it." She giggled again.

After an hour of talking, drinking tea, making jokes, we left, but not before asking Marina to come to the Foundation the next day for an audition. She was very excited.

∽

Marina was already at the Foundation waiting for us when we arrived. Nabi Tanha and Shah Mohammed were there as well, though we had not asked them to come. They just wanted to see Corinne, say hello, find out how far we had advanced, and learn when the project would start.

Corinne was happy to see them, and updated them. She explained that Marina was going to have an audition. She invited them to stay, then she asked Marina to improvise anything that she was comfortable doing. Marina did not know what Corinne wanted. She did not know anything about theatre, nor the meaning of words such as "audition," "improvisation" or "rehearsal." She only knew how to stand before a camera, say a line, and make faces as she was told by the director.

I explained to her the concept of improvisation. She said that she would do a little girl who is in search of a book that, she was told, will answer all her questions about life's mysteries: why one person is poor, why one person is rich, why one person is sick, why one person is healthy, why one person is sane, and one person is mad, and so on.

Before she started, she began to giggle, and could not stop. We all laughed with her, but she continued giggling to a point that it got a bit tedious. We wanted to see what she could do. She noticed that we had stopped laughing. She wanted to stop giggling, but she could not.

She said, "I can't stop laughing, Qais. I don't know what to do." Corinne did not know what to do, either, or how to stop her.

Nabi Tanha suggested that she should do some improvisations about her life, recounting her memories of her childhood. Corinne agreed. Immediately, a cloud swept over Marina's face as she nodded her head.

"I was little. Life was hard. I saw girls in nice clothes holding their parents' hands going from one shop to the next, buying beautiful clothes. I had no hands to hold on to. I had parents, but they lived at the mercy of the passersby. I learned from them how to do the same. Sometimes people gave me some food or a little money. Sometimes they were angry with me for being hungry. Sometimes they laughed at me, especially the kids.

"My feelings for those kids were mixed with happiness and jealousy. I felt happy for them, because they could have everything they wanted. Yet I felt jealous towards them, because I wasn't born with the same chances. Life was a mystery to me. Why one is so poor and another can have everything? Why didn't God create everybody the same?"

Suddenly, she started to cry. We thought she was acting. She tried to continue, but sobs clung to her voice as she attempted to recount one memory after another. Tears rolled down from her eyes. Her whole body shook. I felt very sorry for her. She was touching something within me. Corinne asked me in a whisper if she was still acting.

"I don't think so," I replied.

Abruptly, Corinne got up and hugged Marina. She started rubbing her back, saying softly, "Shhh, shhhh. It is okay." Corinne's two daughters were nearly the same age as Marina. At that moment, Corinne understood instinctively as a mother that what Marina needed had nothing to do with being in a play. Corinne held her for several minutes, and let Marina sob against her chest.

I looked at Nabi Tanha who was wiping his eyes, but not wanting anybody to see. He smiled at me, and walked towards Marina to make jokes with her to cheer her up. Or maybe just to escape painful memories of his own. Shah Mohammed, who could always make people laugh, made some funny faces at Marina, but she could not see them through her tears.

Nabi Tanha said, "Marina, cry, cry. Crying is good for the eyes. In America, people go to pharmacies to buy artificial tears, to wash out their eyes. We have plenty of them by ourselves. We may not have a lot of clean things, but our eyes are the cleanest in the world."

Marina raised her face and looked at him, wanting to believe him. Corinne rocked her back and forth until she quieted. When she made a little giggle, we knew she would be all right.

"From now on," Nabi Tanha said with unusual tenderness, "I will be your uncle, and I will protect you." Marina smiled at him, and whispered, "*Tashekur, Kaka Nabi.*" ("Thank you, uncle Nabi.") Throughout the weeks that followed, Nabi Tanha took that promise very seriously, and did many things to help Marina learn the craft of acting on stage.

Now we had completed the cast. Marina was in.

9

Rehearsals, Act One

Kabul. June, 2005.

In the same weeks when I was helping Corinne cast the play, I was also working with Qaseem Elmi and Khan Mohammed Stanekzai on the script. We were trying to match the lines in the Farsi translation with the English version that Corinne and Stephen had edited. They had made many cuts. In fact, they had made a whole new play out of an old one, even without writing new words. It was very hard for us, though, to line up the two versions, and to make sense of them.

For one thing, neither Qaseem nor Stanekzai nor I could completely understand Shakespeare's English or Dr. Pazargadi's Farsi. And then, to make things more complicated, the names of the characters in the English original had been given Persian names in the Farsi version.

Sometimes we would just look at each other and wonder what we were supposed to be doing. Sometimes we looked at Stephen at his desk across the room. He had no idea what we were going through. He smiled. We smiled. What else could we do?

Still, working with Stanekzai was a treat. Even when he said ordinary things, they sounded like poetry. He spoke the sweetest form of Pashto that I had ever heard. Sometimes I would ask him questions which did not need to be asked, just to hear him give an answer.

When we needed a break, Qaseem and I would arm-wrestle for

a while. He is very strong. But I am very strong, too. I am sure that I pinned him more times than he did me. But he may say the same about himself.

Once in the middle of wrestling, I suddenly understood the meaning of a phrase that had been confusing us all afternoon. I was so excited I relaxed my grip, and he slammed my arm down on the table. I cried foul. But in Afghanistan, there are no excuses, only winners.

Finally, the Dari version of the script was completed. One by one, the pages came out of the printer, each of them looking to me like small masterpieces of calligraphy that promised great things.

Corinne called the actors together at the Foundation to get rehearsals started.

I was excited. I was going to be working with people whose faces I had known only from the television until I had met them during Corinne's workshops. I had worked as a radio announcer for a while, but nobody sees the face of a radio announcer, and I was not famous like these people. This was all very new to me.

When the actors were all seated on the Hazaragi *kilim*, Corinne told them the story of the play. They liked it. Then she announced who would be playing which part.

Shah Mohammed Noori would be Haroon, the King of Kabul, whom Shakespeare had called Ferdinand. Shah Mohammed liked the idea of being a king. For a few moments, it seemed like Nabi Tanha thought that he should be the king, but Corinne gave him the role of Sohrab, whom Shakespeare had called Biron or Berowne, and told him that it was the most important role in the play. That made him happy.

Faisal Azizi was cast as Mansour, Shakespeare's Dumain, and Arif Bahonar was given Sherzad, Shakespeare's Longaville. Kabir Rahimi played a role we called Sikander that we had cobbled together from a couple of lesser characters who act as messengers.

Sabah Sahar was the Princess of Herat. We all knew that she was best for that role. Shakespeare had called her the Princess of France. Marina Gulbahari would play Senober, who had originally been Rosaline. Breshna Bahar was given the role of Maryam, a name not so different from its original, Maria.

Leila Hamgam was asked to play Narges, who was Shakespeare's

Katherine. And Parwin Mushtahel was the lady-in-waiting to the others known as Fatima. Most of her lines came from a male character named Boyet who attends the ladies, but that would not have been possible in Afghanistan. Hence, Fatima.

❧

Then it was time to distribute the script to the actors, and that is when the problems began. We discovered that only Nabi Tanha, Sabah Sahar, Shah Mohammed and Arif could read the script with any ease. Some of the others could read it a little, but they had difficulty understanding the meaning of many of the words and even whole sentences.

Marina Gulbahari faced the greatest challenge. She could not read any of her lines at all. With only a rudimentary education, she was simply unprepared to make sense of Shakespeare's dated vocabulary and poetic allusions. My premonition on the first day I had met her had proven to be correct. But she could hardly be blamed. When she should have been in school like other kids, she had been out begging for food so her brothers and sisters would have something to eat.

My first job as interpreter was to help five of the actors, including Marina, understand the meanings of each word. It was difficult. Sometimes I did not even know the meanings myself. Sometimes I used my two dictionaries. Sometimes I knew the words, but had a difficult time conveying what they meant. Sometimes we just agreed to change an archaic Farsi word for a current Dari one so that we and the audience could understand what we were saying.

The problems started right from the opening lines of the play, spoken by Shah Mohammed as Haroon, the King of Kabul:

HAROON
Let fame, that all hunt after in their lives,
Live register'd upon our brazen tombs
And then grace us in the disgrace of death;
Kabul shall be the wonder of the world;
Our court shall be a little Academe,
Still and contemplative in living art.

Shah Mohammed read it slowly, then looked up with questions in his eyes. He looked at the script once more, but was not sure whether to go on, or start again. He had not been able to take in the meaning of the lines he had read. Nobody else understood them either. He read them again.

And so it went with the others. Breshna Bahar as Maryam was confronted with:

MARYAM
If love makes me forsworn, how shall I swear to love?
Ah, never faith could hold, if not to beauty vow'd!
Though to myself forsworn, to thee I'll faithful prove:
If knowledge be the mark, to know thee shall suffice.

We could work through the wordplay of the lines and find the general sense of what Shakespeare had intended, but that was not the same thing as really understanding what he had written.

Marina as Senober had some of the most complex lines:

SENOBER
They are worse fools to purchase mocking so.
That same Sohrab I'll torture ere I go:
How I would make him fawn and beg and seek
And wait the season and observe the times
And spend his prodigal wits in bootless rhymes
And shape his service wholly to my hests.

When Nabi Tanha read the lines to her, she looked at him blankly. The unfamiliar words she was hearing simply did not mean anything to her.

It was a full week before we finished reading the whole script just once.

During this time, Corinne was anxious to be doing more than just reading. But without knowing Dari, she could not easily be part of the actors' conversations about the script. It had to be very frustrating for her. From time to time, she would interrupt, and ask me what we were talking about. I would explain. She would beg me to move things along a little faster. I said that we would try. But we could not.

∽

After one week, we were ready to start the actual rehearsing. We sat in a circle. All the men were on one side, and all the women were on the other. Every day, Corinne tried to get them to mix together, but no one moved.

The actors started reading the play aloud, with a lot of stumbling over the strange words. Corinne sometimes interrupted to encourage the actors to speak louder, to project their voices. When the actors could not do it properly, she taught them some vocal exercises.

We began to see the challenge we would face by working with actors who had had no training. Only a few of all the actors in Afghanistan have ever had the chance to go to university to study acting or anything else. In Afghanistan, acting is a job people often do when they lack the skills or the knowledge to earn money in other ways.

Once when Nabi Tanha's voice dropped as he was having trouble reading an especially troublesome word, Corinne stopped him, saying, "We have to pronounce the words forcefully, and not as if we are reading them for ourselves. Pretend you are on stage reading for hundreds of people in the audience and…"

Nabi Tanha, who did not welcome being interrupted, mumbled, "I think she is a kind of woman who interferes too much in other people's affairs. I don't know if we can manage to stay and work with her." Corinne seemed to have sensed discontent, and stopped speaking.

Sabah Sahar took Corinne's silence as an opportunity to offer advice to Nabi Tanha. "Don't judge someone by her words," she told him. "Consider what people think of you, not what they say. She thinks well of you. She came all the way from the West to tell you something of her work, which is respected there. You have to take the understanding of the East which is here, and the knowledge of the West that she brought with her. What she tells you is for the play, and it is good to know.

"She has a good eye for details," Sabah Sahar continued. "A director has to notice things, often very little things in order to find out the right move for the scene and remove all the mistakes. And a director's eyes are like a camera, always taking photographs in her mind and always trying to understand what is going on."

Nabi Tanha did not like to be told how to think. "Enough of your philosophy," he said dismissively.

Sabah Sahar was not intimidated. She replied "I would be on your side, if you were right."

Corinne quietly asked me with disquiet in her voice, "Do I need to know what the hell is going on? Qais, tell me what is it?"

Nabi Tanha, who understood English, whispered to me in Dari, "Don't tell her what I said. Just tell her that Sabah Sahar made me better understand what she said."

"Well… nothing special," I said to Corinne. "Sabah Sahar explained exactly the same thing that you just said. That is all."

Corinne unleashed her frustration of the past week at me. "Why did she have to do that, Qais? Didn't you interpret everything properly? Why didn't Nabi understand what I said? Qais, tell me, do you yourself understand what I say? You really have to listen carefully, and tell them exactly what I say. Otherwise it will all be a mess. I don't need two translators. One translator is enough."

I did not know what to say, but I needed the small money I was being paid, so I said, "Yes. I will try."

Every day, there were moments like that. My biggest problem was that I had to translate everything that was said to Corinne. Neither I nor Corinne could stop the actors from arguing among themselves over things she had told them. And I could not translate what they said to Corinne, because when I started to, everyone from every side whispered, "Don't tell her. Say something else." I had to make up something else to tell her, and I was not good at it.

10

Rehearsals, Act Two

Kabul. July, 2005.

We rehearsed the scenes in order. This meant we spent a lot more time on the early scenes, as Corinne introduced the actors to many new ideas about rehearsing, acting and Shakespeare.

The first scene was only with the boys. We were beginning to see what each of them could do.

All of Nabi Tanha's years of training and experience showed in his work. He moved around the playing area as if he belonged there. He knew where to place himself to create visual relationships between himself and the other actors. When he spoke, his words were clear, and always as if he were saying them for the first time.

Shah Mohammed had not had the same kind of formal training. Nabi Tanha often made suggestions to Shah Mohammed on how he should play his scenes. Shah Mohammed would look off in the distance while Nabi Tanha was speaking to him, then nod his head, and do what had been suggested. One thing for which Shah Mohammed needed no help in was speaking clearly. His enunciation was a joy to hear as he always pronounced his words precisely and poetically.

Arif was the most surprising. He had never done theatre before, but from the first time that he spoke his lines, all the other actors stopped what they were doing, and really listened to him. He has the ability to make people pay close attention to what he is saying. His acting is like a magnet that draws attention.

Faisal had had no training, but he watched the other three guys very closely. He quickly figured out what he was supposed to be doing. He was very creative, and full of suggestions on how he and the other boys should be playing their scenes.

Corinne listened to his ideas at first, but he had so many. As the clock ticked down to the end of the rehearsal and his ideas kept coming, Corinne would sometimes get exasperated. Poor Faisal. He would always smile and say, "Take it easy *Khanom-e-zelzela* (Madame Earthquake), it was just an idea." The others would laugh gently. I would interpret it as, "He said, 'It was just an idea.'"

"When I need an idea," Corinne would reply with a sigh as she looked for her place in the script, "I will ask for one. But not every time I give him some direction."

෴

The second scene was only with the girls. From the first rehearsal to the last performance, Sabah Sahar was a one-person rescue squad among the girls, ready to assist anyone in trouble. With a half-smile, a slight raising of her eyebrow, or a tilt of her head, she could help the others remember a line, or guide them to move to some place they had forgotten to go.

Breshna Bahar had energy and good instincts, but sometimes she seemed to want to learn more through trial and error than by taking direction. Still, she was always interesting to watch.

It was a couple of weeks before either Marina or Leila really began to understand the individual words they were saying, but they were still fighting to grasp the full meanings of the sentences. Corinne worked out movements with them to go with their lines. But since they really had no comprehensible lines to which they could attach these actions, they quickly forgot what they were supposed to do.

That became a real problem when we reached the third scene, when the boys and the girls are on stage together for the first time. Marina, as Senober, has a quick exchange with Sohrab. That would go well, but in the next exchange between the two of them, Sohrab would say:

SOHRAB
Lady, I will commend you to mine own heart.

SENOBER
Pray you, do my commendations; I would be glad to see it.

Marina understood that Sohrab was leaving, but was confused when Corinne was unhappy with the gesture she had made as he went, as if she were dismissing a pushcart-man. Corinne tried to help her find a different kind of gesture more suited for a noblewoman. They spent a long time on it. But Marina was at loss to put the newly devised gesture together with the line that was little more than random sounds to her.

In a country like Afghanistan, with its many languages, it is common for people not to understand what somebody next to them is saying. Often people learn a few functional phrases of another language – 'thank you', 'goodbye', 'how much' – even if they do not know the precise meaning of each word. Marina was working in this kind of linguistic borderland, doing the best she could, intuitively presuming that, over time, these odd sounds would start to make sense to her. But for the meantime, her lines could have as easily been in Turkmeni, Pashayee, Uzbeki or some other language.

One day in frustration, she asked, "Why do I have to talk to Sohrab so poetically? Instead of asking him if his soul suffers, why can't I say, 'Are you in pain?'"

While Marina struggled and Corinne explained, the others would get bored. The smokers had to smoke. Corinne hated the smell. She would interrupt her discussion with Marina to complain about it strenuously. The actors fussed right back at her, always several at once. Their message was clear without my having to interpret.

I would try to move things along to the next scene so the clash would not become a brawl.

∾

Corinne and I talked many times about Marina's and Leila's difficulty with their lines. Further complicating things, Marina and Leila did not understand many of the lines that the other actors were speaking either. Hence, they often missed their cues. At one point, we decided to cut some of their lines, thinking that might help. But when it did not, Corinne undid the cuts.

Corinne tried several techniques to get everyone past this stage. One of them seemed to work. She would start each rehearsal by having all the actors sit in a circle and read their lines from the text very fast without any acting. Before long, almost everybody had mastered speaking their lines, and some were even beginning to know theirs by heart. Then Corinne had each person explain the meaning of the lines when they said them. It was a good learning experience for everybody.

Separately, Corinne asked Leila and Marina to explain *Love's Labour's Lost* in their own words, in simple storytelling. At first, they were at a complete loss. Slowly, though, they began to get a sense of what the play was all about. For nearly three weeks, we did these storytelling sessions. Finally, they really did understand *Love's Labour's Lost*, and, perhaps more importantly, they became genuinely excited about it.

∿

The frustrations that Corinne had been feeling began to emerge more often. She spoke more insistently, trying to convey the urgency of the situation in her tone of voice. The actors did not understand her words until she finished, and I had translated them. But they had heard the edge in her voice, and bristled at it. That made them grumble.

Perhaps this was the way directors worked in France, they would say, but in Afghanistan – though we all like to think of ourselves as warriors – we have very strict rules for how we speak to one another. Good manners are considered essential for a good – and long – life. A person who breaks those rules and displays what we consider bad manners will soon see our warrior side.

∿

Every day, the women still sat on one side of the circle, and the men on the other, despite Corinne's repeated efforts to get them to mingle. Some of the women did not even look at the men when they were speaking to them. Corinne invented a series of exercises to force them to interact.

One involved a ball that they had to pass around the group, but always to somebody of the opposite gender. Her goal was simply to get them to look at each other as they passed the ball, thinking that perhaps that would help break down barriers.

∾

The weather kept getting hotter and hotter in a way that was unusual in Kabul. We could not comfortably work indoors, because we did not have enough space in the old salon, nor in any of the Foundation's other rooms, even though some of them were large. Nor could we comfortably work outside in the garden, because it was just too hot. Everyone started getting cranky, the way people do in Kabul when the heat and dust rises, and there is no good air to breathe.

Then, every day we had a sick actor, either from food poisoning or dehydration. At one time or another, everybody had diarrhea. Even me. Even Corinne. This is life in Kabul.

To Corinne's dismay, her sessions at the Foundation could not begin until after 4:00pm. The actors all had jobs. Many of them worked for government agencies. And Arif, of course, was attending classes at the university.

Corinne became upset when actors arrived late. There was not a single day when everybody came on time. The actors would shrug their shoulders and say: "Traffic jam." "I was not feeling well, and did not want to come, but at the last minute I decided to come." "Traffic jam." "My mother was sick, and I had to take her to the doctor." "Traffic jam." "We had some guests, and I had to make them tea." "Traffic jam." "I had a lot of school homework." "Traffic jam." "We had a lot of work in the office." "Traffic jam." "I was sick, and I went to see a doctor, and here is my medicine." "Traffic jam." "I went to see a sick friend." "Traffic jam."

Corinne hired a driver to pick up the actresses from their jobs or homes to try to get them to the Foundation on time. She implored the actors to come when they were supposed to. Most did, but not always.

We could work only until 6:30pm, or at the latest to 7:00pm. The women had to be home before dark, or their neighbours would start gossiping about them. In Afghanistan, a woman is either a "good woman," which means she does what her husband or family expects her to do, or she is not. There are few gradations in between.

With such a short time to rehearse every day, Corinne became more and more frustrated. She had not expected to need a full week to get the actors through the first reading of the script. She had had no way of understanding how complicated and time-consuming it would be to work through an interpreter.

Corinne was always wanting to say something to the actors. The actors were always wanting to say something to Corinne. Sometimes she spoke emphatically to the actors when they did not seem to understand what she was saying. Inevitably, the actors spoke just as emphatically back at her. Stress was apparent on everyone's faces.

One afternoon, Corinne complained to me that the actors were not listening to her. I told her a joke.

"Eighteen years ago," I said, "there were some Russian farmers in Maidan Wardak province. They came to teach farmers 'capacity building,' but the Afghan farmers killed the Russians farmers. The media went and asked the Afghan farmers, 'Why did you kill the Russian farmers?' The Afghan farmers told them, 'Oh, the Russian farmers were good people. They were doing a good job, but they did not behave well. They tried to tell us what to do.'"

She did not understand my joke. "What has farming to do with this?" she asked with annoyance.

"It is too early to tell them what to do. Behave nicely to them, otherwise you will have the same fate as the Russian farmers." She smiled, and said I was silly.

I persisted, saying, "Start little by little, step by step, drop by drop. Don't try to do too much at once."

Maybe I should have thought of a different joke. That one did not work. She kept on raising her voice to the actors. Suddenly, a couple of actors would feel insulted and quit in the middle of a rehearsal. Corinne looked at me pleadingly, asking me to help. I had to find a way to get them back. We had gone through so much to find them; we could not afford to lose them now with only five weeks before the first performance. Anyway, I had no idea how we could find replacements for them.

I would take a deep breath, pump myself up with a manufactured positive energy and speak to the departing actor to encourage him or her to come back. This happened many times. Sometimes, I failed at first. But after a while, I succeeded, and they came back. Until the next time they quit.

Once, Nabi Tanha said, "Qais, you are a lot younger than I, but do you know that you are a millionaire?"

I looked at him quizzically, not understanding what he meant.

He continued, "You're a millionaire in your spirit, and strong as well. You own a lot of patience for your age. God save you from the evil eye."

Breshna Bahar would quit about once a week, saying in English, "I don't want to work. I quit. It doesn't worth it." Then she would complain that she was being paid very little for all this aggravation, even though the actors were each receiving $600 for being in the show, which was a lot more than most of them were making on their jobs.

On such occasions, I would say, "Breshna jan, a true actor does not care for the money, but for quality. You are playing Shakespeare here. Not every actor can play Shakespeare, not even famous ones." This always worked, and she came back. It worked for some of the others, as well.

My success in bringing the actors back, though, really had very little to do with me. All the Afghans involved in the play, and, in fact, everyone in Afghanistan, is under unending stress from the moment we wake up in the morning until the moment we wake up the next morning. The stress does not even end when we sleep. Will a bomb explode tonight? Will a telephone call come about a relative who has been killed? Will it be safe to send the children to school in the morning? It just does not stop.

When I would take the actors aside, I was giving them a moment of quiet and calm where they could release their anger at the lives we were being forced to live. Maybe they would shout about something

Corinne had said to them that they did not like, but really they just had to vent about something – anything – because everything else had become too much.

They all wanted to be in the show. They all wanted to be good actors. They all wanted to learn what Corinne could teach them. They all knew that they had to let go of what had ignited their anger, and return to the rehearsal.

Perhaps the heart of the issue may have been in Corinne's astonishing drive. Even when I was sitting quietly under a pomegranate tree before a rehearsal, I always knew when she had arrived. A special kind of energy seemed to move ahead of her. She was not noisy or trying to attract attention. It was just that the air changed and became charged with possibilities when she entered.

Sometimes, though, this single-minded forcefulness seemed to act like a spark that would unintentionally set off an explosion.

Corinne once asked me if I thought the problem was that she was a woman giving orders. Maybe this was true for the men on some level, but it was not an issue for the women, and some of them quit more often than the men. Even more than Nabi Tanha.

∾

Nabi Tanha was both a trouble maker and a trouble solver. There were times when he would suggest something worth considering to Corinne about a scene or a movement. Corinne's habit, unfortunately, was to cut him off in midsentence since she did not know what he was saying, and say, "No," before he had finished explaining his idea.

The next minute, he would quit, and encourage Shah Mohammed and Faisal to quit too. He was their leader. They did as he did. I had to go out into the dusty street as they walked away, and plead with them to come back, while Corinne busied herself with the girls.

Nabi Tanha would say, "Do you know the reason for my quitting?"

"No," I would say each time, even though I knew exactly what he would say next.

"Tell her that this is not how we talk in this part of the world. We listen to one another, even if we know that the other person is completely wrong, and then we express our ideas and thoughts in a polite and respectful manner. We don't cut people midsentence. If she were a man, I would have smashed her face by now."

"Okay," I would reply in a consoling voice, "but please come back. We are running out of time." And one way or another I managed to bring him back. And with him came the other two guys, who had not really wanted to leave and were always happy to return.

Sometimes I had to ask Parwin to help me get Nabi Tanha back. Parwin could always find the right words to say. She would say, "Nabi jan, don't be angry with Corinne. She is one of those people who talks first, then thinks about what she just said. Have you heard of the expression 'Your mouth is your best friend if you have control of it, and your worst enemy if you don't'? Her mouth may be an enemy to her, but she means good to us."

Nabi Tanha always listened to Parwin, because she was the second oldest among the actors, and everybody respected her.

But Nabi Tanha would always say to me in a tight voice, as if I were the one he was angry with, "Qais, you have to teach Corinne some manners. You speak her tongue, and spend more time with her than us."

"Okay, Nabi jan, I will teach her some manners."

When I tried to teach Corinne some manners, she would always cut me off in midsentence and start complaining about the actors, about their being childish and immature. I listened and waited. My Grandfather had taught me to make patience my master. Deep down I knew that, in the end, she would ask me for my help and advice.

Though she never seemed to want to hear what I was saying to her, a few days later she would end up doing more or less exactly what I had suggested. It was a strange way of doing things, but I could live with it. I took my pleasure from knowing that, though I knew very little about Shakespeare or theatre, my ideas were good and being used.

11

Tea With Shakespeare

Kabul. June and July, 2005.

Our limited time for rehearsing each day was made even shorter, because we had a half-hour break at 5:00pm to drink tea and eat some cake or cookies that the Foundation provided.

There were many times during the break when the actors argued with each other for no particular reason. That occasionally led to fierce fights. A few times, Corinne and I had to separate them, and bring peace between them. Then, like a mother to her children, Corinne would go into long explanations about why they should not fight. The actors listened and whispered to each other, making fun of Corinne, a woman, telling them not to fight.

They would say, "She came from France, and she thinks she knows the solutions to all our problems," and everybody would laugh among themselves.

When Corinne saw the smiles on their faces, she thought she had made peace between them, and felt happy at having solved their problems, and started the rehearsal again.

∾

Corinne kept coming up with new ways to get the men and the women to interact, which until then was happening only when they were having arguments.

One day, she suggested that we play volleyball on our breaks, with each side having some men and some women. Volleyball is practically the national sport of Afghanistan. Everybody plays it. Even if they do not play it well, they enjoy it. The Foundation had a net at one end of the garden.

Despite the heat, we went there on our break. All the women stood on one side of the net, and all the men on the other. Corinne watched in despair from the terrace. She called out, "Faisal and Shah Mohammed, you change places with Breshna Bahar and Leila." Everybody laughed, but nobody moved.

It took a couple of days for some of the women to feel relaxed enough to play on the same side as the men, but they soon liked it. In fact, everybody liked it so much that they did not want to stop playing at the end of the break, and come back to rehearsal.

$\sim$

Besides providing time for fighting and the pleasure of complaining, the tea breaks gave the actors an opportunity to talk among themselves. A frequent topic was Shakespeare. Everything about him was new to them. Being in a play was new to several of them. Many of the actors were new to each other. Their discussions, which sometimes grew surprisingly heated, were a time of discovery for all of them.

One day as we were pouring the tea, Shah Mohammed asked the group, "Who wants to share his impressions of Shakespeare?" Shah Mohammed had a way of relating to the group like he was everyone's favourite uncle. He treated us all as if we were his extended family. But no one replied to his suggestion.

"OK, let's start from Qais, then," Shah Mohammed said. I groaned inside. Since I had to do the talking for everybody throughout the rehearsal, I looked forward to the tea break to rest my voice.

"Well," I said, "Shakespeare makes a vivid impression on anyone who makes the effort to understand him." Then I bit into a very big piece of cake that required a lot of chewing. I put one hand to my mouth, and waved the other around a little, hoping that somebody would interrupt. I was learning about acting with my new friends.

Nabi Tanha, may his sons be blessed, took over the conversation. I could relax now.

Nabi Tanha spoke like a thoughtful and well-educated *mullah*. He drew himself up and started using his hands to amplify his points. His hands are very finely-boned. He moves them with great grace. They speak eloquently by themselves, but Nabi Tanha, who usually talks in the Kabul street dialect, was matching the language of his gestures with very formal and poetic Dari. His eyebrows would rise to emphasise words he thought were important and make him look very wise.

"Shakespeare brings utter silence into your consciousness. The way he uses words, they rush like a small river from somewhere far away, and bring sadness and happiness, restlessness and restfulness into you. They make you feel sorry for yourself and everyone else, and vice versa. The words leave you motionless, and take you into a deep, pensive silence."

Nabi Tanha was crouched between a kneeling and squatting position. His thin, expressive body was becoming a part of what he was saying.

"When I am reading his words," Nabi Tanha went on, "I want to glue my eyes to the lines until I become blind. I want to take in every part of every word and know all its meanings." He relaxed back onto his *toshak*. "But I don't think our people will understand Shakespeare. Shakespeare plays with words, while our people played with guns for the past three decades. Some days, I think that doing Shakespeare is a waste of time."

Sabah Sahar looked at Nabi Tanha with cool-eyed approval. "You're very good," she told him, "even better than I thought. But I won't let you tell us that 'doing Shakespeare is a waste of time.' People in this country understood Shakespeare thirty years ago. Why can't they do so now? Do we go forward or backward?

She adjusted her head scarf, which had the effect of focusing attention on her large, carefully made-up dark eyes, and continued. "You have to think of the words you say before they come out of your mouth, and ask yourself if they are worth saying. You judge very quickly before you take your time, like these crazy politicians we have. You can see the result of their wrong judgments in all these years of war."

Sabah Sahar spoke with the directness of someone who is accustomed to people paying attention to what she says.

"We have to believe that our obligation is to replace guns with words. These wars in our country were made by dangerously narrow-minded people who preferred weapons over words. We have to think that human nature can be improved. Guns kill you. Words can save you."

Nabi Tanha had been challenged, and was ready to fight. Shah Mohammed saw that, and tried to tamp things down before they erupted. "Enough out of both of you," he said gently. "Are you going to give the rest of us a chance to talk?"

Sabah Sahar eyed him with an air of jovial superiority and prodded Shah Mohammed saying, "I will shut up, if you have anything to say that is worth hearing."

Shah Mohammed smiled and replied, "All I wanted to say was 'let's drink our tea before it gets cool.' I am starving. I want to eat, and I am politely waiting for you and Nabi jan to start so I may. But instead, you two accelerated like a broken car that no one can stop." Everybody laughed, and that crisis was diffused.

∾

There were many, many more discussions about Shakespeare during the breaks. It was a time when the actors felt free to express themselves. Being Afghans, they spoke at some length. Being Afghans, we enjoyed that, and listened to them, and then we replied at some length.

Nabi Tanha would often start the conversations. He had emerged as the strongest member of the group, though Sabah Sahar and Breshna Bahar would probably not agree with that. But then, they rarely agreed with Nabi Tanha on anything anyway.

One day Nabi Tanha turned to Kabir, the quiet one, and asked him what he thought of *Love's Labour's Lost*.

Kabir started by saying that, "Shakespeare was a man of art in the way he used words. He loved his art with all his being. I can see that. Maybe you can as well. That is why when I read his plays, his poetry rises into my heart and brings a kind of feeling to me that I can't explain."

Everyone was very quiet. We were interested in hearing what Kabir had to say. Not only was he the oldest member of our group, and thus deserved our respect, he was not by nature a talker. He smiled a lot, but said little.

"By listening to Shakespeare, those with guilty consciences suffer. If you suffer from a wound, it can be healed. But if you suffer from your conscience, it cannot. He knew that."

Kabir spoke confidently. But in his eyes was a sense of worry, lest the insights that Shakespeare had given him, and which he found precious, would be dismissed by the others. He kept on speaking, though.

"The wounds that we suffered in all of the fighting here, they will be forgotten in a few years. But by doing this play, we will bring our suffering to those with guilty consciences who are still in this country and ruling us. That is why we must invite them, the warlords. In fact, we can change our visible wounds to invisible wounds that hurt from the inside out."

This was the most we had ever heard Kabir say. We were amazed. Nobody wanted to say anything after he had spoken. We all sipped our tea silently for a few minutes. He retreated into his teacup, and said no more. Nabi Tanha was intent on keeping the conversation going, though, and he turned to Arif.

"I didn't know much about Shakespeare before I came here," Arif said. "I'm learning so much about him and his work everyday. Each time I read something that Shakespeare has written, I get the feeling that I understand everything that he is saying. The next day, though, I discover something else in those same words that I didn't know the day before. And the next day, one more thing."

Arif is powerfully built, but agile. Often, before our rehearsals, he would be bending his legs in unusual ways, or stretching like an athlete before an event. His voice has a melodic quality that invites listeners in.

"Shakespeare's words bring a warm light into my heart, and he charms me with his tales. His storytelling kills all my life's sorrows, and surrounds me with soft arms which bring joy. Sometimes I feel puzzled. I ask myself how such a man existed four hundred years ago? How come we don't have more like him now?

"You know, we are dead even though we are alive," Arif continued, his voice floating like a soft flute. "If we die tomorrow, or after a week, no one will talk about us anymore or remember us. But he is still alive, because of his plays."

Shah Mohammed was beaming with approval at Arif's words. "Well done, Arif!" he exulted, as Faisal said "Wah, wah, wah, wah…" which is how Afghans show that they think somebody has said something worth hearing.

Nabi Tanha looked around. "Who else? One of the ladies? Marina Gulbahari! What do you think of this play and Shakespeare?"

Marina looked startled to be asked. She was the youngest among us, and had expected all the older ones to speak first. But with all the eyes looking at her, she started speaking, and did not even giggle.

"I don't think I have anything worth saying," she said shyly. "When I read Shakespeare, all of a sudden I found his words were many colours. Some were red ones or green ones or black ones and many other colours."

Marina's face is like a fast-changing sky. Sunshine one moment, and dark clouds an instant later.

"I am trying hard to understand them. But when I find myself unable to read them, they pinch me, and bite me, and sting me, and make me want to cry. But I don't cry, because it will make everyone unhappy. So, I giggle." And she did.

Parwin looked at Marina very sweetly. "We won't let these words bite or sting you, Marina jan. You are the youngest one in the group. We will help you understand the colours. You can just ask us or Qais when you don't know the meaning of words." Marina felt the good feeling in Parwin's words and grew calm.

Nabi Tanha was nodding. He was taking his new duty as Marina's uncle very seriously, always trying to protect her and make the way smooth for her. Marina, perhaps because she was so young, was especially shy when talking to the men. But ever since Nabi Tanha had encouraged her to call him uncle, the tension that kept her shoulders tight would ease when she was talking with him.

After she had been coming to rehearsals for a week or so, he told her that Shah Mohammed and Faisal were like brothers to him. If they were his brothers, then that meant that they, too, were her uncles, and she should feel at ease with them. Slowly, it worked. But she would tighten up again when she had to speak to the other men. Nabi Tanha continued to work quietly with her. Before long, she was even able to speak with Arif and Kabir as well, helped by the warm and open personalities of both.

Nabi Tanha leaned towards Parwin as he spoke to her, saying, "You give Marina good advice, Parwin jan. Now it is your turn to tell us what you think. It has been two weeks we have been here, but we haven't heard a word from you. At least tell us why you are doing this play, for the play's beauty or for the money?" Everyone chuckled.

Parwin blushed, and looked around at everyone, then spoke very quietly. "Nabi jan, will we be rich when we do this play?" The chuckles broke into big laughs that ceased as Parwin continued in a serious voice.

"I am here for two reasons. First, it is my career choice to be an actress and to be here. Secondly, I am very excited to be doing such a great play. I have never had this chance before. I find Shakespeare full of distractions, of distances, of borders and of encumbrances more than all the other playwrights I have read. He understands everything about the human mind.

"Even though most of his plays are fables about royalty," she went on, "he always comes back to the real life, and prefers being ordinary. His message is always 'Honesty.' It is a simple message but it takes time to understand him. You have to find the deeper meaning of his words."

Parwin broke off, as if suddenly self-conscious from everyone's attention. Absent-mindedly, she looked around the garden for her young daughter whom she always brought with her to the rehearsals, as she had no one at home to care for her. The little girl was always beautifully dressed and well-behaved. She was sitting under a pomegranate tree, watching us with big eyes. As soon as Parwin registered that she was all right, she continued.

"To make a long story short, Shakespeare is a gesture in theatre that you can never hide. He is the gesture you can never forget. By doing *Love's Labour's Lost*, our audience will be surprised at the rhythm in his poetry. And they will find the answer to many of their unanswered questions in his words."

We were beginning to understand that Parwin was a person with deep thoughts, even though she did not share them often.

❧

Nabi Tanha turned the conversation to his sparring partner, Sabah Sahar.

Sabah Sahar lit a cigarette, and inhaled slowly before she spoke. Only a strong woman would smoke a cigarette outside her home, or even inside. She was letting us know that she saw herself as being as important as Nabi Tanha within this group. She blew her smoke into the air as she carefully chose her words.

"Shakespeare brings caravans of ideas to his audiences. He is the best in capturing the fragrance of life, even if it is sour. His deeper message is for those who lack imaginations, who are sick with a poverty of thought and yet are in power.

"I have found *Love's Labour's Lost* to be the story of narrow-minded people, who impose huge limitations on everyone with no ultimate benefit to anyone. This play is very clear in showing that putting limitations on our lives is like building a huge wall in the middle of a road on which all of the people must travel to go everywhere, as the Taliban did. Sooner or later, though, that wall will be knocked down. People will force their way past the limitations, even if it costs them their lives."

Sabah Sahar thought about things in a way many Afghans did not. She had an important job with the Ministry of the Interior, but she never said exactly what that was. A few times she mentioned that she had visited other countries for meetings representing the Ministry, as well as for business related to her film and television work. She also referred to her three children once or twice, and said that she had to take care of her house like any other woman. She was very private about her private life, even though she also had a very public life as an actress.

Once when I was walking along the road in front of the Ministry of the Interior, the gate swung open and a black BMW with tinted windows came roaring out, nearly hitting me. Then I heard someone calling my name, "Qais? Qais, is that you?"

I looked back at the car, and saw that it was being driven by Sabah Sahar, looking at me through large dark sunglasses from her lowered window.

"Wow! Is that you, Sabah Sahar?" I asked.

"Yes. Where do you need to go? I can give you a lift."

"Okay," I said, "but do you want me to ride inside the car, or were you just now trying to bounce me up on the grill to be your new hood ornament?" She laughed as I climbed in, and gave her directions to my home.

One day she joked about the dark make-up she always wears around her eyes. She said, "I can act like a princess or a servant. It doesn't matter to me. It is my job to do both, but I don't want anyone to touch my make-up! I want my make-up for both of my parts, princess and servant." Then she laughed.

She told me once that she had been trained to jump out of planes with a parachute. Now she was asking Shah Mohammed to give us his opinions on Shakespeare.

∾

Shah Mohammed rocked forward and backward a few times, as he always does when he is getting ready to speak. "First of all, I have to say that when the wind moves like a comb through a field of wheat, it leaves a hundred trails. Shakespeare is like a strong wind that goes direct to the human mind and conscience, and it stirs answers that we have been seeking."

Everyone nodded in agreement. Shah Mohammed's face gets very animated when he speaks. His mop of dark hair adds to the drama of his words as he moves his head, looking intently first to one person, then another as he speaks. He never just says words, he always speaks to someone and makes them feel that what he is saying is especially for them.

"Shakespeare can describe the cruelty of this world by making someone a prince or a princess, then showing how ignorant these people are. Then he shows that being ordinary can be much worthier, maybe even easier. He tells us, 'Don't yearn to be wealthy or well-known, because they may bring unhappiness.'

"The deepest message in this play: let's enjoy every colourful season, the golden earth, and the blue sky, and listen to our hearts, not to our negative emotions and feelings. If you conquer the whole

The ladies of *Love's Labour's Lost* prepare to perform.

From the left, Marina Gulbahari practises a grand gesture, as Breshna Bahar sits to check her make-up, Sabah Sahar oversees the proceedings as she will soon be doing as a princess on stage, and Leila Hamgam gives her costume a full swirl to make sure it is hanging properly, while the daughter of Parwin Mushtahel, one of the "mascots" of the production looks on.

Before each performance, as they donned their elegant costumes designed by Shahla Nawabi, the actresses practised the songs they would sing in the show.

Marina Gulbahari is known to many for her performance in the title role of the award-winning film *Osama*, directed by Siddiq Barmak. Though she has made several other films since, *Love's Labour's Lost* was her first appearance on stage. She played her role with the commanding presence and witty sophistication of a stage veteran.

Photograph by Kate Brooks

Haroon, the King Of Kabul, played by Shah Mohammed, reads a proclamation announcing that he and his three noble friends have taken an oath to avoid contact with women for three years so that they may have time to study and improve themselves.

The three nobles played by Faisal Azizi, Nabi Tanha and Arif Bahonar make their way down the stairs of the partially ruined Queen's Palace that is set amid elegant gardens in Kabul, designed four centuries earlier by the Mughal emperor Babur, a near contemporary of Shakespeare.

Shakespeare set his comedy in the Kingdom of Navarre. In this production, however, the setting was shifted to the Kingdom of Kabul.

Photograph by Kate Brooks

The Princess of Herat, played by Sabah Sahar and dressed in green, sits with her ladies to discuss the curious circumstance in which they find themselves. They have arrived in Kabul only moments after the King and his nobles have sworn to have nothing to do with women. But Afghan hospitality requires that the men receive these ladies who have come to discuss a matter that is causing tension between their kingdoms.

Hand-woven kilims were laid in the dust to create a playing area. The King's *takht*, or throne platform beyond the women, is draped in carpets hand-knotted in the Afghan-Turkmen style.

While the women spoke among themselves, the audience kept growing, using the steps behind the playing area as seats and eventually filling them completely. The actors could not use them to exit at the end of the play.

Photograph by Kate Brooks

The director of *Love's Labour's Lost*, Corinne Jaber, watches as the young nobles grapple with their burning desire to talk with the newly-arrived women despite their oaths. With her is David Elliot whose memorable hospitality in the grand salons at the Qala-e-Noborja, which he had restored first, brought together many of the Afghans and foreigners who worked together to make *Shakespeare in Kabul* happen.

Photograph by Kate Brooks

Despite their oath, each of the men finds a way to secretly send love letters or poems to the woman he most admires. When the messenger is confused and delivers them to the wrong ladies, uproarious confusion follows.

Love's Labour's Lost marked the first time that men and women had appeared together on stage in Afghanistan in decades. Every performance was given knowing that objections might be voiced. None ever were. The audiences responded enthusiastically.

The actors performed in Dari, one of the main languages of Afghanistan.

Photograph by Kate Brooks

The young nobles hug in joy after confessing to each other that each has been secretly trying to contact the women on his own, and deciding they should pursue the ladies deliberately – much to the delight of Faisal Azizi (second from left).

In the scene that follows, they disguise themselves as Indians to keep the ladies from recognising them. That scene always set the audience roaring with its interpolation of familiar Bollywood songs into Shakespearean verse.

Photograph by Kate Brooks

The romantic adventure in the garden of the King of Kabul suddenly turns serious when the women discover they must return to Herat at once, resisting the pleadings of the men to marry them immediately. Rather, they set as a condition that the men must contemplate their marriage proposals for a full year. Only after that will the women consider them.

The fact that it is women who decide the outcome of the story was one reason why *Love's Labour's Lost* was particularly appealing to director Corinne Jaber.

From the left, Arif Bahonar, Shah Mohammed, Leila Hamgam, Sabah Sahar, Marina Gulbahari, and Breshna Bahar – who when offstage is one of the highest ranking women in the Afghan security services – and Nabi Tanha.

Photograph by Kate Brooks

Parwin Mushtahel
Photo by Christopher Morris

Kabir Rahimi and Mustafa Haidari
Photo by Qais Akbar Omar

world, it means nothing. But if you conquer your heart, it is every-thing. Some people seem to have forgotten the meaning of life. Life is cruel. If you take one side of life, the other side falls down. Life has two faces, one smiles and laughs. We must strive to show that face." Indeed, that is how Shah Mohammed always seemed to approach life himself.

Sabah Sahar raised her eyebrows with an impish smile, and said to him, "I am glad you're more optimistic than your friend," meaning Nabi Tanha.

Nabi Tanha ignored her. Instead he looked around and asked, "Who's left? Oh Faisal! You should have spoken to us before everyone else. You're our poet. Tell us your thoughts on *Love's Labour's Lost.*"

Faisal always looks to his left before he speaks, then clears his throat. He did that, and said, "In a roundabout way, *Love's Labour's Lost* makes fun of our recent history, the Taliban, who ruled us with their nonsense and cruel rules. *Love's Labour's Lost* is all about their nonsense rules."

Faisal always has a fuzz of whiskers. Maybe he has nowhere to shave. Maybe he is just trying to be ready if the Taliban come back.

"All these fancy words, though, in *Love's Labour's Lost* are beyond the understanding of our people. Look at us, we barely understand them ourselves. We have to help our audiences understand that each word has many meanings. We have to be extremely clear with these words without changing the text."

Shah Mohammed has the face of a teacher. Nabi Tanha has the face of a prince. Kabir has the face of a good man who suffers in silence. Faisal has the face of someone you want as your best friend. In fact, he greets everyone with "My best friend!" He continued.

"Firstly, Shakespeare's way of using words is not our way. Secondly, we are not as educated as he was. Thirdly, we as actors have never had such an extremely difficult text. At least I haven't. I personally have never faced such a strong playwright who can admire someone in the beginning of a sentence and destroy him at the end of it with just one word. Every word is powerful."

Nabi Tanha looked pleased.

Faisal continued, "From the first day until now, we are getting better every day. We have to make sure that Marina and Leila understand their lines, so they can make our audiences understand them. Otherwise a tiny mistake by one of us will cause distractions to the rest of us. I have a suggestion: someone must come every day thirty minutes early, and help them understand their lines. Who will volunteer to do this?"

Everyone started explaining why he or she could not. One said, "It is already difficult for everyone to come on time." Another said, "I have to be at the office until three o'clock." A third said, "I have a transportation problem." And so it went. There was no one available to help Marina and Leila.

Nabi Tanha looked at me and said, "That only leaves you, Qais jan. Maybe you should do it." He knew that on many days I came early to the Foundation to enjoy the garden. That was supposed to be time for myself, but I wanted Marina and Leila to do well. So I agreed. From then on, I and sat with them every day, and every day they had a better understanding of what Shakespeare wanted them to say.

Often, we met at the Foundation. But sometimes we went to a small restaurant in Shahr-e-Naw Park which had a private garden. I held the script like a school teacher, and asked them to say their lines. In between mouthfuls of pomegranate or watermelon ice cream, they got the rhythm of the poetry. The unusual words started to make sense, and they began to memorise them. Breshna Bahar's daughter Wazhma, who is close to Marina and Leila in age, came with us many times, and helped them when they stumbled over words that still eluded them.

One day Leila's father, Hanif Hamgam, was at the Foundation on business of his own. He saw us as we were rehearsing on the grass. Later, while we were having our tea break, he came and spoke with me quietly for a few minutes.

"Qais jan," he said to me, "Leila is your sister. You are like my son. Protect her like you would protect your sister."

"Of course," I said. I felt very honoured. Hanif jan is a rare voice in Afghanistan who challenges public officials every week on his programme *Zang-e-Khater* (The Alarm Bell). With very sharp and funny jokes, he puts into words what many Afghans want the politicians to hear. Now he was telling me that I was like a son to him.

Then we shook hands, and I asked him to have some tea with us, but he had to go. He is a very busy man. God has given me five sisters of my own. From the first day of rehearsals, though, I thought of Leila and Marina as two more. And after I met Wazhma, she became another sister. I knew my obligations to them, and took them very seriously. This is the Afghan way.

❦

When we had serious discussions during our breaks, I did my best to interpret what was being said for Corinne. But the actors sometimes said so much so quickly that I did not always manage to translate everything. Also, no one waited for me to finish interpreting one thing before they said the next. After all, this was the break and their own time, not a rehearsal. They just kept on speaking. I did get the main points across to Corinne, but she knew she was missing a lot, and that made her unhappy.

She was keenly interested to hear what the actors were thinking. She wanted to get to know them better. Sometimes later as we drove home to the old fort, I was able to go back and fill her in on who had said what. Sometimes that made her feel better, because she finally understood what had been discussed. Sometimes it made her annoyed, because she felt she would have liked to have added something if she had known what was being said.

Corinne tried very hard to help the actors understand what she wanted from them. I could see that she was a good teacher. If only everyone had spoken the same language, it would have been easier and better. But there were times when Corinne would try unsuccessfully to explain something to the actors, only to run out of patience and walk away. She would come back after ten minutes, and start again. But there were times near the end of the day when she got completely fed up, and just left the Foundation, and went home.

On the way home, she would call me from her car, and ask me to work with the actors on their lines, because she worried that though they could say them by heart, they still did not always understand them.

On the days when Corinne went home early, the actors were like kids when the teacher leaves the classroom. They would make jokes with each other, laugh, chat and drink tea. When I insisted that we sit on the floor and read their lines aloud from their script, or recite them from memory, they did so, but some of them only reluctantly. Some of them still did not seem to have fully grasped what we were aiming to do.

Once they saw that I did not interrupt or criticise them, though, they relaxed a bit. The more we worked together on our own, the fewer mistakes they made. In fact, they really started to enjoy their work. When the time came for everybody to go home, they continued working in the car, helping each other when somebody made a mistake, and showing real enthusiasm.

The next day, they came back, eager to demonstrate the moves they had worked out the day before. Corinne, though, was trying to keep to a schedule, and knew we were way behind. She needed us to move on to something else. That made the actors feel small. They started acting weird all over again, threatening to quit, or not following Corinne's directions, or criticising her, or complaining, or going to the bathroom and spending a long time there.

I could see that Corinne's mind was racing with ideas she wanted to share, but the actors were discovering this curious world of Shakespeare at a very different pace. Corinne was on a deadline. The actors were on a journey of discovery.

And I was in the middle.

12

The Meaning of Love

Kabul. June, 2005.

Despite all the challenges, the progress that the actors were making in these weeks was nothing short of historic. They were pushing aside thousands of years of social customs, as well as thirty years of trauma. Each day, each one of them was able to drop his or her defences another little bit and connect to one of the other actors. It was a series of small actions which by themselves may have appeared insignificant. But, taken together, they were huge.

One of the basic elements of the play, though, was not making any sense to the actors: the idea of 'love.' They had lines that were full of passion, but put no passion into their performances.

Nabi Tanha was saying lines as Sohrab that explained why love is a reason for marriage:

SOHRAB
And I, forsooth, in love! I, that have been love's whip;
Regent of love-rhymes, lord of folded arms,
The anointed sovereign of sighs and groans,
Liege of all loiterers and malcontents,
O my little heart:
What, I! I love! I sue! I seek a wife!

But he seemed to have no sense of the power of the words.

Arif, as Sherzad, was speaking of Maryam, played by Breshna Bahar, saying:

SHERZAD

O sweet Maryam, empress of my love!
Vows for thee broke deserve not punishment.
A woman I forswore; but I will prove,
Thou being a goddess, I forswore not thee:
My vow was earthly, thou a heavenly love.

Arif was oddly diffident as he spoke. Shah Mohammed as Haroon, King of Kabul, was meant to be going crazy with love when talking about the Princess of Herat:

HAROON

So sweet a kiss the golden sun gives not
To those fresh morning drops upon the rose,
As thy eye-beams, when their fresh rays have smote
The night of dew that on my cheeks down flows:
Nor shines the silver moon one half so bright
As doth thy face through tears of mine give light;
Thou shinest in every tear that I do weep:
O queen of queens! how far dost thou excel,
No thought can think, nor tongue of mortal tell.

None of the boys projected any sense of romantic feeling behind these very romantic words.

Corinne tried to explain how men and women on her side of the world develop feelings for one another. When the four young nobles see the beautiful women from Herat, they are supposed to have these feelings. That is what causes them to break their vow. She could not understand why no one seemed to understand what it was like to fall in love.

She had noticed how everyone enjoyed big discussions during the breaks, so one day she decided to have a discussion on what love is, instead of a regular rehearsal. She asked all the actors to sit in a big circle. By now, the men and the women all sat among each other. That in itself was a big sign of progress.

She said to them, "This play is called *Love's Labour's Lost*. If we are going to tell this story, we need to understand what love is all about." Then she asked each actor to say what 'love' meant to him or her.

"Love has many meanings," Arif said helpfully. "But I know love best by its spiritual meaning." Like most Afghans, Arif's family had chosen his wife. He had not had the same experience as the young nobles in the play.

"Love," he said, "is a deep feeling of affection towards something or someone. Those kinds of feelings originate from certain qualities of that thing or person which cause your soul to respond positively to it, and to strongly want it."

"Give me an example," Corinne said.

"For example, I love to pray and do *zikkur* (a religious ceremony)."

"I entirely agree with Arif jan," Nabi Tanha said. "And I want to add the meaning of physical love. Love is a feeling of intense desire and attraction towards a person. In short, the emotions that lead to sex and romance."

"Sexual passion," Shah Mohammed interjected, serious as always, but he still made everybody laugh a little.

"That is right," Nabi Tanha said. "And also an intense emotional attachment, as well as affection and attraction towards that person."

"Endearment?" Shah Mohammed asked.

"Yes, that is what I mean," Nabi Tanha affirmed.

Nabi Tanha sounded as if he had come to understand what Shakespeare had written about. Now it was up to Corinne to help him connect the ideas he was expressing to the character he was playing. She also had to get some of the others involved in the discussion

"Let's ask one of the girls," Corinne said.

Breshna Bahar said, "I agree with both Arif and Nabi. But I think the meaning of love cannot be explained by words, because our vocabulary is not extensive enough to explain ideas such as love, soul, mind, spirit, essence, or conscience. I think that love means an incomparable feeling of affection and solicitude towards someone or something which you have a strong desire to own."

Breshna Bahar, like many Afghans, must have had some Greek

ancestors. When I went to Athens a few years later, I saw many ancient statues whose faces had profiles like hers. They had expressions of total serenity that were frozen in marble forever. As Breshna Bahar spoke of love, her usually animated face had the same calm look.

"What Breshna jan just said about love, it makes it sound like a selfish word," Leila chimed in. "When you love, you have to own it, or your love will make you suffer. If that is so, then love is a selfish word, and the act of love is a selfish act."

"Then what is love?" Breshna Bahar challenged sharply. Her calm had gone in a flash.

"Maybe I don't know, but to me love means a feeling of warm personal attachment or strong attraction to another person," Leila responded.

Shah Mohammed intervened again, adding "Something earnest, like affectionate dedication that implies more selflessness and abiding feelings."

"Exactly!" Leila exclaimed.

Before Breshna Bahar could say anything else – she was making the face she always makes when she is getting worked up – Corinne asked Parwin: "Parwin, you tell us."

"It is simple. Love means to care, to desire in a respectful manner, to be pleased with and please, to give pleasure and gain pleasure. It can be an intimate sexual relationship between a man and woman. And we use the word 'love' to honour that."

"But that is not a complete meaning of love," Faisal challenged. "What you just said is a definition of love from a Western point of view."

"True, true!" everybody exclaimed.

"How so?" Corinne asked as she looked at everyone curiously. "What is your Eastern definition of love, Faisal jan?"

"Westerners express love along the road, in bars, at home, on the roof, anywhere, without any regard or respect for it. My definition for love is fondness and devotion of a *lifetime* for something or someone in a respectful manner."

Nabi Tanha joined in. "Everybody knows some sweet lines to say to a girl to make her like you, but real love is in here, in the heart. I have seen in Hollywood and Bollywood movies where the guys tell the girls, 'I looked at a flower, and thought it was the most beautiful thing I'd ever seen until I met you.'"

Shah Mohammed chimed in sarcastically, "Or, 'The only place I can meet you is in my dream, and I don't want to wake up.'"

Dramatically, Breshna Bahar added, "I just want you to be happy, even if I'm not the reason for your happiness."

Leila made a cheap Bollywood girlish gesture, which made everybody laugh hard, as she said, "Don't worry, my love, if you fall, I won't let you hit the ground."

Arif looked at Leila and swooned, "You are my heart, my soul, my treasure, my today, my tomorrow, my forever, my everything!" Everybody laughed.

"Oh, yeah, like I would believe that," Leila was fast to reply. Everybody laughed even harder than before.

Faisal adopted a theatrical manner and looked intensely at Breshna Bahar. "A candle may melt, and its fire may die, but the love you have given me will always stay as a flame in my heart."

"Shut up, idiot," Breshna Bahar cackled, but delighted nonetheless with his flirting, even if it was only done in jest. Everybody else roared with still louder laughter.

Parwin wanted to say something, but Nabi Tanha interrupted.

"My point is," he said "that these lines don't mean anything. Everybody is capable of making such seductive lines all day long. Real love is something rare, and it can't be easily found. Real love is not some kind of a clever line that I can say. Real love is two hearts with one beat. Real love is commitment to a lifetime devotion, and loyalty in all times until death separates them.

"In the West, people have built a different concept of love over time. A boy looks at a pretty girl, and falls in love, and vice versa. They fall in love with their appearances. But the surface beauty doesn't last very long, only to a certain age. What then? You spurn your 'beloved', because he or she is not beautiful anymore? And it seems this is exactly what is happening in the West. That is why the rate of divorce is so high, and it is getting higher and higher every year.

"If that is what you call civilisation, then civilisation is a monstrous disaster. What about our prophets' times? If your concept of love in the 'civilised' world is expressing your feelings in public, then does it mean that our prophets never experienced love, because they lived in an earlier time, and were not civilised?

"Have you read the story of Prophet Joseph and his master's wife? It is in the holy books sent by God. She fell in love with Joseph's good looks. And we all know the consequences. That is what is happening in the West. That is why the 'falling in love' thing only lasts for a limited time, while in this part of the world, love is true.

"We may not love our wife or husband when we first marry, because it is an arranged marriage. But, over time, it grows into a real love. I'm not saying that every arranged marriage works out for the best. There are many failed ones, but not as many as yours, which you call 'love.'"

All the actors were nodding quietly in agreement. Afterward, Corinne mentioned that the discussion had been one of the most revealing moments of her time yet in Kabul.

"What about you, Qais jan?" Corinne asked me.

"I agree with everyone?" I said, diplomatically, because I was tired of translating all that they had said.

"Even with Parwin?"

"Yes, even with Parwin."

"He agrees even with Parwin," Corinne said to everyone. She was trying to start a little fight. She likes to do that. It is her way of having fun. In some ways, she is like an Afghan.

Shah Mohammed said, "Maybe he has seen too many Western movies."

"Maybe," I said, smiling noncommittally.

Corinne looked at Marina, "Now, Marina jan, you tell us what you think."

She turned red and said, "I haven't experienced love yet, and I don't know. Maybe you can ask me this question in ten years."

"Okay," Corinne smiled, "I will remember to ask you this question in ten years."

Corinne looked at everyone and suggested, "Let's talk about 'Hate.'"

Everybody exclaimed in one voice, "No!"

"Why?" Corinne asked, surprised at the outpouring.

"Hate is what our country and its people have been cursed with for the past three decades!" Arif said strongly. For once, the smile that had a permanent residency in his eyes was gone.

∽

From that day, Corinne started to listen more. Of course, sometimes she was still impetuous. And sometimes the actors sputtered in response. But a new feeling had entered our rehearsals.

We were now at the end of the third week, exactly halfway to our first performance. Finally, everyone was feeling comfortable with the script. Half of the actors had memorised most of their lines. They were making some mistakes, though, and mispronunciations. Sometimes they added their own words to the text, which changed the meanings of whole monologues.

Since Corinne did not speak Dari, she was unaware of this. She was happy just to hear words coming from their mouths. I kept a script in my hand, and helped them to use the right words.

Every day we were getting better, better than the day before. Slowly, we were making Shakespeare's story our own story.

13

Behind the Scenes

Kabul. June, 2005.

Corinne met the actors every afternoon. But during the rest of the day, she was busy working on other aspects of the show.

One of these was getting costumes made. She had heard about a designer named Shahla Nawabi who was then in Kabul. One day Corinne went to visit Shahla at her family's home in Shahr-e-Naw. Shahla had been born in Afghanistan, but her family been forced to leave when Shahla was seven years old.

Her family is related both to the former king of Afghanistan, Zahir Shah, and to the Khan of Qalat, the ruler of the Balouch people who have no country to call their own, but whose lands are spread across Afghanistan, Iran and Pakistan. Those connections made it dangerous for her family to stay in Afghanistan after the Communist government replaced the king. Many of Afghanistan's intellectuals and professionals disappeared without a trace during that time.

After the Taliban were driven from Afghanistan at the end of 2001, Shahla was among the first Afghans abroad to return home. She had become a successful businesswoman in England. She used the skills she had learned there to set up a construction company in Kabul.

She had never run a construction company before, but she had managed the women's side of a leading British department store, Turnbull and Asser, for seven years. She knew her way around a balance sheet. And she was determined to do something useful in Kabul that women were not expected to do, and to help rebuild the country.

When Corinne met her, she was building courthouses and clinics in various parts of Afghanistan. She used one part of her family home in Kabul as her office. She and Corinne met for tea in a sitting room whose walls were decorated with sepia-toned photographs of notable ancestors.

Corinne laid out for Shahla what she was doing with *Love's Labour's Lost*. Shahla immediately understood the vision, and agreed to be part of it. The budget for costumes, though, was tiny, just a couple of hundred dollars. Still, with a bit of imagination, Shahla felt she could come up with something that looked royal and eye-filling. After so many years of designing clothing and jewelry for London, she was excited to be doing something Afghan.

She suggested that the costumes should draw from the style of clothes worn by the Turkmen tribes in northern Afghanistan. Turkmen women are less likely to be as heavily veiled as those from other groups such as the Pashtuns. A stage full of *burqa*-covered women was grimly funny to imagine, but would present a real challenge to the audience.

Turkmen women typically wear their headscarves over small round caps that vaguely resemble a crown. That would make the girls appear more royal, than if they were simply draped in headscarves. Turkmen women also wear very elaborate jewelry, and the girls could do the same to further emphasise their characters' positions. Better still, Turkmen people are not shy about wearing bright colours, as others in Afghanistan are.

For the boys, Shahla proposed that they wear a simple white *shalwar kameez*, the basic outfits worn by most Afghan males. They could then liven them up by sporting elaborately decorated dark velvet waistcoats. These would be available at reasonable cost in the bazaar. The King of Kabul would be given a very fancy turban, and the three others would wear brightly-coloured round caps. They would tie woven sashes known as *cummerbunds* around their waists.

Shahla made several trips to the large fabric bazaar across the Kabul River in the area known as Mandawi. Though not quite a covered bazaar like many domed bazaars in Central Asia, the streets of Mandawi are narrow, and the awnings of the shops cover them from one side to the other. One street is lined with shops selling dried fruit and nuts. Another sells fighting and singing birds, along with hand-crafted cages for them. Another has *burqa* shops, with their walls covered in *burqas* of many colours, lengths and head sizes. Another is stacked with hundreds of the black-and-white cotton headscarves that every Afghan man wears.

Shahla made her way into the heart of the bazaar where the fabric sellers keep meters and meters of brightly-coloured cloth on long rolls. Although Afghan men and women dress in muted tones in public, Afghans fill their homes with bright, sometimes garish, fabrics that are often used as window curtains.

Women wear richly hued dresses to wedding parties, which for many women are one of the few occasions when they are allowed to go outside their homes. It is at weddings where they get their news, look over prospective brides for their sons, and have a chance to dress up. Much of the brightest fabric of Mandawi ends up in wedding party dresses.

Shahla understood both how Afghan audiences would expect royal women to dress, and how to adapt that to the needs of the play. She had seen many productions of Shakespeare in London. *Love's Labour's Lost* was giving her an opportunity to join together two parts of her life.

She asked the cloth salesmen to spread out one bolt after another. They realised very quickly that she was a woman who knew exactly what she was looking for, and responded enthusiastically. She laid one colour on top of another to see how each complemented the other. Her goal was to create something that looked much richer than the meager budget seemingly allowed by selecting colours that worked especially well together.

A dark velvet for a long skirt for the Princess of Herat was accented by a green and gold apron, bodice and veil. Her ladies would be in long skirts or *kameez* blouses and baggy *shalwar* pants in shades of dusky rose, mustard yellow and deep fuchsia heading towards violet. The veils, attached to multi-coloured Turkmen caps, would come down over the shoulders almost to the knees, and lend a sense of grace, she felt, especially as the girls made their entrances and exits.

Shahla had to settle for imported synthetic fabrics for the most part. She would have loved to use Afghan silk, especially since most of it is produced and woven in Herat, the home of the ladies of our *Love's Labour's Lost*. The silk would have draped more diaphanously, and added a level of grandeur.

All the women's costumes would be richly embroidered in traditional Turkmen patterns. In a curious irony, the embroidery, which would have been prohibitively expensive in London, was available in Afghanistan at a lower cost than the cloth itself.

Though the action of the play takes place over several days, Corinne and Shahla agreed to give the ladies only one costume each. This was at odds with the Bollywood norm where an actress may change outfits a dozen times in a single production number. But they were concerned that audiences unused to theatre might have problems following the characters if their appearance changed too often. This was also a way of stretching the limited budget to make the costumes as elegant as possible.

Shahla gathered some seamstresses and got them cutting and stitching.

∾

Hashmat Ghani Ahmadzai is the titular leader of the Kuchis, Afghanistan's Pashtun nomads. What better man, then, to ask for a Kuchi tent? We needed one to accommodate the Princess of Herat and her ladies while they were encamped in the King of Kabul's garden.

Kuchi tents are woven from black goat hair and stretched over wooden frames. They provide shelter from the sun during the hottest part of the day, and a place to retire at night. At their best, they are utilitarian. Corinne, however, said that the tent should be highly decorated.

Perhaps Hashmat understood that. From somewhere, he found a white, six-sided tent made of canvas that did not look at all like anything a Kuchi would live in while herding sheep. But it was perfect for *Love's Labour's Lost*.

He also gave us some magnificent tent hangings that exactly complemented the Turkmen accent of the costumes. The tent took up a relatively small amount of ground space, which proved critical in the garden of the Foundation where we wanted to fit in as large an audience as possible.

We had expected to raise the tent as part of each performance. But after we put it up once and saw how complicated doing that was, we just left it in place. A real Kuchi tent would have been even more difficult, unless we had real Kuchis raising it, like my cousins who live as nomads still, following their herds of sheep and camels all over Afghanistan from March to October, searching for high mountain pastures that are kept green in the heat of the summer by the run-off from melting snow packs. And living under tents.

Hashmat was then busy campaigning for a seat in the Afghan parliament whose elections would be held two weeks after the play was performed. A few years later, his brother, Dr. Ashraf Ghani Ahmadzai, who had served as Finance Minister, would be one of the candidates in Afghanistan's presidential election, and become known to people around the world.

Hashmat is a living history book on Afghanistan. He runs a trucking business that keeps many Kuchis employed in the modern equivalent of their ancient tradition as caravan leaders and traders.

"The Phoenicians controlled the sea routes," he says, "but the Pashtuns controlled the land routes." That is how a Semitic tribe like the Pashtuns found their way into the place that they named the Land of Abram, or Afghanistan, after our great patriarch. But that is a story for another day, and best heard from Hashmat jan.

∽

Meanwhile, we contacted Rahim Walizada, one of the most innovative young carpet designers and producers in Afghanistan. He had lived in New York for ten years, and had come home to Afghanistan at the end of the Taliban era. He was now making carpets with designs like no one in Afghanistan had ever woven before.

Afghans had never heard of an artist named Mark Rothko whose paintings Rahim had seen in New York. The simple squares of colour that Rothko placed, one against another, excited Rahim. From the moment he first encountered them in the Museum of Modern Art on Fifth Avenue, he saw them as carpets, not paintings.

Rahim displayed his creations at a shop he set up at one end of Shahr-e-Naw, away from all the other carpet traders. The foreigners came there in large numbers to admire and buy his unique creations. His brother-in-law, Mujeeb Siddiqi, was kept busy running the shop while Rahim was working on new designs or placing his carpets in design centres and high-end shops around the world.

As part of their business, they gathered up many beautiful old rugs that they repaired, cleaned and resold. Rahim let us borrow several of these, along with some old woven cushions. We used them to cover the *takht*, the throne platform, where the King of Kabul would sit. With Rahim's carpets, our bare wooden platform was immediately transformed into a king's palace.

∾

I was in charge of finding props, such as musical instruments and a teapot.

I got the musical instruments from Robert Kluijver. The Foundation had some *tabla* drums and a harmonium, the small two-octave organ pumped by hand which is a part of musical performance all over Central and South Asia. The biting rhythms on the *tabla* create instant excitement. The harmonium, with its mysterious, reedy sound, adds a level of seriousness and beauty.

I borrowed the teapot and some Afghan-style cups without handles from an Englishman who lived in the old fort where my family lived. I just grabbed them one day when he was not at home, and I was in a rush. I was sure he would not mind. We had used them every time I had had tea in his rooms.

I never thought to mention that I had taken them to him in the days that followed, and did not know that he was looking everywhere for them. When he saw them being used by the actors during the first performance, he almost jumped out of his seat and screamed, "Those are mine!" How was I to know that they were some kind of rare porcelain?

I assured him that they would be returned in perfect condition after the last performance. And they were. But I watched them very carefully whenever the actors picked one up in the show, and prayed that nobody dropped one.

∽

And then there was Daoud. No one behind the scenes was more helpful. Officially, his job was just being Corinne's driver. But, despite a limited education scratched together in refugee camps in Pakistan, he was a natural-born therapist who solved many problems that were not his obligation to solve.

Perhaps it was his stunning good looks, or his ability to laugh in a way that makes other people laugh. Perhaps it was the joy he takes in speaking to everybody, hearing what is going on in their lives, and then knowing with whom to share what he has heard.

Perhaps it was the half-dozen grey hairs in his always well-combed, thick, black hair, which make him look very dignified and cause people to ask his advice.

Early in the day, when Corinne was coping with heat and dust and an impossibly long list of things to accomplish, he would buoyantly shuttle her around Kabul, using many alleys and lanes that not even the donkey drivers know. Hours later, when Corinne was exhausted, and sometimes discouraged, he would whisk her from the Foundation to the old fort faster than any armoured convoy, all the while generating a soothing presence that could take the edge off anybody's anxieties, even without his saying a word.

Daoud became a fixture of *Love's Labour's Lost*. He sat in on many of the rehearsals. He played volleyball, and drank tea with the cast on their breaks. He learned most of their lines just from hearing them everyday, and could prompt the actors when they faltered, but in a way that made the actors laugh and not feel self-conscious.

When he had finished driving Corinne around all day, he still had to come back to the Foundation and take the girls home, except for Sabah Sahar and Breshna Bahar who had their own cars. On these drives home, he would always tease Marina in a way that was gentle, but just bordering on what Afghans would consider vulgar. He would say something to her like, "Now that you are famous, you must have a line of boyfriends waiting to marry you, all of them good-looking and rich and sophisticated."

Marina always sat in the backseat where the windows were tinted so no one walking alongside the car would recognise her. She would slap Daoud on his shoulder, and complain to me in the front seat, "Look, Qais, he is so rude to me. If one of my brothers or my father hears such things, they will beat him, and they will probably beat me too, for letting him say such things." Then she would giggle.

Daoud loves to sing. He comes from a family of well-known singers, and has a sweet voice of his own. Sometimes he would sing to Marina.

The banter would continue until we reached Marina's house, the first stop on our nightly journey home. After she got out of the car, Parwin and Leila would sweetly take Daoud to task, saying, "She is so adorable! Daoud jan, don't tease her too much."

"Okay," he would say. But we knew he would find something else to joke with her about the next day. One time, though, he told Parwin and Leila very seriously, after Marina had gotten out of the car, "She is like my little sister. I respect her like a sister, and would do anything to protect her if anyone even looks at her in a bad or unclean way." We knew he meant it.

I was the last passenger he dropped off. Then he headed home across the city. Daoud lived in a far corner of Kabul, in an area called Kart-e-Naw. For any other driver, it would have taken an hour to get there. Daoud could make the trip in half the time. And singing all the way.

14

"This Theatre of Heaven"

Kabul. August, 2005.

When the foreigners started pouring into Afghanistan after 2001, they discovered many things that we had always known about. One of them was the magnificent gardens constructed more than four hundred years ago by Babur, the first Mogul emperor of India.

The gardens had been badly battered in the recent years of war. The opposing factions led by Ahmed Shah Massoud, Gulbuddin Hekmatyar and Hezb-e-Wahdat each unleashed hundreds of thousands of rockets at each other. Many fell into the gardens. In several places, the high mud-brick walls around the perimeter had been pulverised, leaving large gaps. Old trees were cut down by desperate Kabulis needing firewood for heat and cooking fuel. The fountains stopped running.

Babur had come to Kabul to lick his wounds after he had been forced out of his homeland in present-day Uzbekistan by family feuding. He created several gardens while he was there. His favourite, he wrote in his diary, was this one on the west-facing lower slope of the Sher-e-Darwaza mountain overlooking a branch of the Kabul River.

He stayed in Kabul long enough to regroup his armies, and recapture his fighting spirit. He went south to India where for the next three centuries he and his descendants would be known as the Moguls or Mughals by Indians mispronouncing 'Mongolians.'

Babur died young at Agra, only four years after conquering northern India. He never returned to Kabul, but left orders that his body should be brought back for burial in his gardens there. He had never missed the chance to send instructions from India for their upkeep.

The Moguls maintained a strong presence in Kabul throughout their years ruling India. Second sons and nephews who did not vie to become emperor were often rewarded with Kabul. Kabul may have lacked the imperial grandeur of Agra or Delhi, but its ruler controlled the important trade routes to Persia and China that passed through there, and profited from them handsomely.

After Babur's death, it was some fourteen years before his descendants returned his remains to Kabul. When they did in 1544, they laid him in a simple grave open to the sky, as he had requested in accordance with his pre-Islamic Mongolian traditions. Sixty-three years later, his great-grandson, the emperor Jehangir, visited Kabul, and placed a headstone over Babur's grave and built a marble prayer platform nearby.

By then, the era of constructing grand Mogul tombs was well established. Jehangir's son, Shah Jahan, who would one day build the Taj Mahal, came to Kabul in 1645 and erected a small marble mosque on the side of the grave facing Mecca. Taking inspiration from Babur's wishes, the mosque is open on three sides.

By 1857, the Moguls were gone from India, and an Afghan family named Durrani set themselves up as a monarchy in Afghanistan. The Durranis kept the eleven-hectare garden around Babur's grave for their private use. One of them, Abdur Rahman who became king in 1880, built several new structures in the gardens.

One of these was a large and fancy pavilion for his third wife, Bibi Halima. It became known as *Qasr-e-Malikha*, the Queen's Palace. It was constructed in a corner of the garden at its highest point. The palace had a large central section, flanked by two smaller wings. It sat on a high terrace above an enclosed garden three times the size of the palace itself. A high wall pierced by arches stretched between the wings and completed the garden's enclosure. A grand gatehouse in the garden's lower corner allowed the queen's curtain-draped carriage to be driven into the palace grounds with all her retinue unseen. For a generation or two, the royals enjoyed the palace in privacy.

Times changed. The royal family moved to a more modern palace in the centre of Kabul's Shahr-e-Naw, the New City. In 1933, all of the gardens surrounding Babur's grave were opened to the public, and became a favourite destination for Kabuli families. Many times my own family went there for picnics on Friday afternoons before the fighting took all that from us. With my grandfather, my father, and all his brothers and their wives and children, we often had fifty close relatives sitting around one tablecloth.

Even before the fighting, the buildings in the garden were beginning to decay. The grave of Babur, the little mosque nearby and the Queen's Palace were left open to the winds. But like Babur, the garden was given a second chance to rise again. Its lifeline came from the Aga Khan Trust for Culture, an organisation committed to restoring imperiled historic Islamic structures. Starting in 2002, the Aga Khan Trust for Culture placed the Bagh-e-Babur at the centre of its comprehensive plan to restore dozens of historic structures in Kabul and elsewhere in Afghanistan.

Overseeing the restoration was a South African-born architect, who had trained at Cambridge University, and had worked in several Islamic countries before coming to Afghanistan. He has been living in Afghanistan for more than twenty years and speaks Dari fluently. His name is Jolyon Leslie.

By 2005, under Jolyon's guidance, the fortress-like walls around the Bagh-e-Babur had nearly all been rebuilt. New trees had been planted, both fast-growing ones to provide some greenery for now, and others like those that once had spread a sheltering crown against the sun.

Hundreds of men from the neighbourhood of squatters' houses that rise in rows up the mountain behind the gardens had been hired to do the work. Many had been farmers before they had been made homeless by the fighting. They were happy for the chance to make things grow again. They brought with them the wisdom passed down to them, and made the once-devastated landscape bloom again. Other workers were helping to rebuild the Queen's Palace, hauling bricks up ladders to make the walls rise anew.

Nowhere in Afghanistan was the optimism of those days more visible than in Babur's beloved gardens.

∽

The idea of doing a performance of *Love's Labour's Lost* in the Bagh-e-Babur emerged from a conversation between Corinne and Jolyon who had come for dinner one evening at the old fort. About a week later, Corinne and I went to the Bagh-e-Babur after our rehearsal at the Foundation. We arrived as the workers were finishing for the day, and the sound of the *azan*, the call to prayer, was filling the evening air.

We tried to enter through the main gate at the gardens' low end, near the river. However, its impressive thick plank doors six meters high were shut tight. We had to keep on driving along the garden's massive, turreted walls to their far end, and then turn up the hill until we came to another gate farther on.

The road there was filled with old men in turbans, teen-age guys in T-shirts, and kids in anything that fit them more or less. Some women wore *burqas*, but most did not.

Daoud was driving and singing. As we eased along the potholed road, he softly sang love songs to the women we passed. Below the rim of the tightly closed windows, his hands made gestures of affection. He was steering the car with his knees, guiding us past buses with their riders hanging out the doors and off the back, and push-carts hauled by Hazara labourers who looked too small to move such heavy loads.

We swung through the upper gate and into the gardens. I had been to the Bagh-e-Babur on a wintry Friday afternoon a couple of years earlier, and it had looked bleak and desolate. Now, my first reaction as we drove through the high arches of the gateway was utter amazement.

Where had all these trees come from? There were rows of them on each of the cascading terraces that led down the hill to the main gate below. Who had planted all these roses, now blooming? The transformation was astonishing. So, too, was the panorama across the Char Deh valley where a spur of the Hindu Kush mountains was bathed in golden, evening light.

Jolyon was talking with one of his Afghan engineers when he saw us. I had heard his name many times, always spoken with respect by foreigners and Afghans alike. But this was the first time I was meeting him. With an accent more British than South African, he welcomed us and started telling us in a soft-spoken way about the buildings and what his organisation was doing with them.

He suggested that we wander in the garden to find a spot that would be suited to a theatrical production. We started out on the terraces with their grassy slopes that offered natural arena-style seating. But with all the new trees, views of the actors would be blocked, except in some very small areas. We needed a place that was larger and more open.

Jolyon led us up to the Queen's Palace, where restoration work had started only a few weeks earlier. We entered a large doorway faced in white marble that was turning pink in the late afternoon sun. It led into a covered passageway that, in turn, opened on to an expansive, elevated terrace beyond. Workmen were coming and going through the passageway, hauling buckets of rubble out, and carrying wooden planks in.

Building materials and rubbish were scattered in piles across the terrace, as well as in the garden below. But the space had a grandeur despite the ruins that surrounded it.

At either end of the terrace were the two wings of the old palace that had managed to remain partially intact. Between them, where the heart of the old palace had stood, only five towering arches marked what had obviously once been very grand rooms.

The wing on the far side of the terrace had not suffered as much damage as the other parts of the building. Inside it was a marble-tiled *hamam* – a steam bath – whose decorative plaster had somehow remained unscathed by the ravages of time, war and neglect. It was a small gem of a room. Very little imagination was needed to conjure the ladies of the court lolling on the warm stones, as the soothing heat made them feel fresh.

The terrace itself was fronted by a row of five half-round buttresses built with stone blocks. They looked like the battlements of a castle. Wide stone staircases flowing down from the terrace to the enclosed garden below curved around the ends of the battlements as they descended.

"The terrace is a perfect stage," I said to myself. I could easily see the high arches providing both a grand backdrop, as well as places for entrances and exits.

Across the bottom of the garden, the high wall that closed off the Queen's Palace from the outside world had many small arched openings. Through them, breezes from the valley below could sweeten the air within. From them, the ladies of the court had been able to watch people in the garden without being observed. In a society where being a good story-teller is a social obligation, such vantage points are essential for gathering the tidbits around which a tale can be spun. We would be continuing an honoured tradition, I thought, if we performed our play here.

∽

The tour was finished. Corinne was talking now, thinking aloud as she visualised how the play might be presented in the ruins of the palace. She moved back and forth across the terrace, then behind the five high arches, then down the sweeping staircases to the garden, and then back up again.

She asked questions. Jolyon and I offered opinions, as did Stephen, who had arrived shortly after we had. New questions. More opinions. Ideas were flying and then discarded and replaced as the creative process flew like kites in the evening wind.

There were problems. The terrace was truly a natural stage, but it really was too high. The garden below, however, was gouged by the remains of an old fountain. Jolyon insisted that the hole could be filled and the rough terrain around it could be smoothed. That was hard to visualise.

We went back up the stairs. We walked around the terraces in front of the wings. Stephen proposed that the girls make their initial entrance riding camels. He felt it would be very dramatic if they entered from the gatehouse. The camels would be brilliantly decorated, as they often are, with canopied seats, elaborate weavings and tassels and bells.

For the next several weeks, he tried to find camels. He went to the large livestock market at Kampani to look for drivers who might understand what he had in mind. He talked to some Kuchis he saw passing through Kabul with a mother camel and her newborn. He even checked with the Kabul Zoo, but all to no avail. In the end, the camels were dropped. It was decided that if one of them were to panic and charge the audience, the results would have been dramatic in a way no one wanted.

Finally, Corinne made her decision. If Jolyon was absolutely sure he could get rid of the fountain – he was – and could smooth out the earth in the garden – he could – then Corinne would have the actors perform on the garden level with the battlements as their backdrop. The battlements truly made the space in front of them look like the garden outside the castle of a king.

The palace and its garden were a love poem that Abdur Rahman had written for his favourite queen. Only a king could compose on a scale like this. The labours of his love may have been scarred by time, but they had not been lost. And we would use them to the fullest.

∾

We walked out of the Queen's Palace enclosure through the carriage-high arches of the royal gatehouse. We stopped for a few minutes to look at the pieces of carved marble temporarily stored there. A team of translators were working its way through the inscriptions on them, trying to reassemble the fragments into the complete stones they once had been. Most had been shattered by the rockets.

With the sun now settling on the tips of the mountains, we strolled along the upper terraces of the Bagh-e-Babur to a small pavilion that Abdur Rahman had built in the centre of the gardens. A verandah runs around it. On the side where the slope falls away to the terraces below, the verandah seems to float in the air. The expansive eaves of the roof extend over it, supported by more high arches, but wooden this time.

We stood for several minutes there admiring the view, as Jolyon pointed out the *caravanserai*-like structure that his team was building just inside the main gate below. A real *caravanserai* had stood there in centuries past. Indeed, the narrow roadway between the gate and the river is one of the many strands of the fabled network known as the Silk Road.

Just beyond the pavilion was the mosque constructed by Shah Jahan. The marble for the mosque had been delicately carved along its edges into crescents of stone lace. Six elaborate finials crown its flat roof. Jolyon showed us the inscription that Shah Jahan had ordered to be placed there. In part it reads:

> …only this mosque of beauty, this temple of nobility, constructed for the prayer of saints and the epiphany of cherubs, was fit to stand in so venerable a sanctuary as this highway of archangels, this theatre of heaven, the light garden of the Godforgiven angel king whose rest is in the garden of heaven, Zahiruddin Muhammad Babur the Conqueror.

"This theatre of heaven." I liked that. I felt it was a good omen.

15

Rehearsals, Act Three

Kabul. August, 2005.

Finally, the actors were on their feet. Corinne was blocking their positions. Some of them moved a bit clumsily, though, and Corinne had to explain basic techniques, such as not blocking the audience's view of other actors when something important is happening.

Marina was still puzzled about what theatre is. She asked me one day, "Why bother with theatre? Why not make a movie? It is easy to make it, easy to buy in shops and easy for anyone to watch, any time they want to watch it."

She was very hardworking, but was having a very hard time. She had more lines than either Leila or Breshna Bahar, and in the first weeks whenever it came time for her to speak, she looked at everyone in wide-eyed fear before opening her mouth. When she spoke, she had pronunciation problems. And when she had to look at the script, she had reading problems. Sometimes, she had giggling problems. She had crying problems a few times. When she started giggling, nobody could stop her, because everything seemed funny to her, until something reminded her of the Taliban times or the war. And then no one could stop her crying.

One day she asked me, "Was Shakespeare a Talib kind of guy? Why is he so strict with all these rules?" I explained that Shakespeare had died four hundred years ago, long before the Taliban. She giggled for a moment, and then her eyes moistened briefly before she started giggling again.

As the weeks passed, she became a much-loved and much-respected member of our little company. Marina was never late, or sick, or complaining. She was always in good spirits, always trying her best to do a good job. We have a saying in Dari, "She has a back for work." That was an apt description of Marina. Also, small acts of kindness were part of her every day. When she had a quiet moment, she took it upon herself to look after Parwin's daughter. Or she would help the Foundation staff in some way. She generated a sense of being very happy to be in the company of the other actors. They could feel that, and they returned her good feelings.

We began to understand, too, that her fame from the film *Osama* was a mixed blessing. It had given her a chance to travel and see other countries, but even in her own neighborhood she sometimes had to listen to unkind words hurled at her from passersby who denounced her for acting. For her, a *burqa* was a welcome disguise, and she often wore one when she left her house.

∾

The Foundation had built a stage at one end of its garden. They used it every weekend for concerts of classical Afghan music, and planned to make it the main stage for the upcoming Afghan Theatre Festival.

For our play, though, Corinne wanted us to perform in the centre of the garden, with the audience seated around us on three sides. Most of the action would take place on carpets laid out in the grass.

The raised stage, however, had about the same amount of playing area as our actors would be using on the grass. We started rehearsing on it. I began to notice that when some of the actors climbed its three steps, something about them changed. It was as if they were leaving Kabul and entering Shakespeare's world. From the moment Arif stepped on to the stage, he became a young noble. Sabah Sahar became a princess.

As Corinne moved around the stage with the actors, guiding them to their positions and explaining their movements, she was more relaxed than she had been in the previous weeks when she had been forced to sit and wait for the actors to work their way through the script with me. That frustration had given way to the kind of dynamism that comes from doing something creative. She became the funny and happy Corinne again, and that made everyone else relax as well.

She worked very closely with the women. She took into account what they did not know or could not do, and looked for ways to help them use the skills they had. She was especially gentle with Leila and Marina, even when they messed up. Sabah Sahar kept her distance from Corinne personally, but she understood Corinne professionally, and did what was asked without any argument, and did it well.

Breshna Bahar was like a human tornado, often twisting her lines in ways that threw the others off. Corinne would be unhappy with the others, not knowing what had caused the problem. We would then have about five minutes of backing-and-forthing with me in the middle trying to straighten things out. The actors' voices would start rising, and Corinne's voice would deepen. That was her serious voice.

Then Breshna Bahar, who can be very funny, would crack a joke that made all the actors burst out laughing, and we would go on to the next thing, with Corinne looking perplexed but content.

∾

One day, Parwin arrived late, shaking. She told us that she and her husband and their children had been locked out of their house because she was in the play. They lived with her husband's family, as is the custom in Afghanistan. Her neighbours were saying that she must be a prostitute since she came home every night at dark, or soon after. Now his family was angry after hearing the gossip, and would not let them stay there anymore.

The family was from Khost province, one of the most conservative areas of Afghanistan. When relatives came to Kabul to visit, Parwin was terrified that they might see her on television doing advertisements. She would play DVDs nonstop. But with the spread of television coverage around the country, her husband was now getting phone calls from outraged relatives asking him why he was allowing his wife to bring dishonour on the family by appearing on television.

One day she was walking home from the bazaar when a man came from behind her on a bike and punched her in her back. "I fell down in the street really badly," she told us. "I still have a pain in my leg, because he punched me so hard. I was with my little son, and I was crying." When she reached home, her husband noticed that she was limping. She told him that she had slipped on the road. She did not want to worry him.

Parwin also told us that she had been receiving death threats during the rehearsals, but had not wanted to tell us about them.

A couple of weeks earlier, she had told us, "I wanted to be an actress from when I was in school, but because of my family I could not do it. Now I am married, and my husband decides what I should be, and what I can do. He is happy with my work."

But often she had trouble remembering everything she was supposed to do in the play.

She had said on one occasion, "You have to understand me, Corinne. How many things should I do at once? I am thinking of my son. Who will take him home from the kindergarten? What should I cook for tonight? Acting here, listening to your explanations, understanding my lines, keeping my eyes on my daughter who is wandering in the garden there, thinking that she may hurt herself. And I have no idea who is in my house now, whether my husband is still at work or if he will come home late tonight. Do we have electricity tonight? If we don't, how can we sleep without a fan? We have so many mosquitoes. I don't know why people don't have eyes to see me and understand me."

And now the eviction. She told us about it in her quiet voice, but we could see she was deeply frightened. She explained that she had to leave right away to go with her husband to find a new place to live. She apologised to Corinne and the rest of the cast. Corinne was sympathetic, and thanked her for coming to let us know. She asked if she needed any help from the police. Parwin told her that that would make things worse.

She left, but she was back the following day, saying only that they had found a place to stay for now.

From then on, her son and daughter came to nearly every rehearsal, as there was no one at home to care for them. When we rehearsed, they watched us intently. No matter how many times we did a scene, they watched it as if they were seeing it for the first time. Her daughter was a smiler; her son was more serious. They were always very well dressed, and never rolled around on the ground the way most kids would do, and get their nice clothes dirty.

∾

Love's Labour's Lost was now beginning to take shape, but slowly. The hardest scene for the actors was the third scene, where the boys and girls are on stage together for the first time. There are a lot of movements. The dialogue must be fast. The focus shifts from one set of characters to another several times. The King of Kabul and the Princess of Herat have to discuss a complex, unpaid loan. It provides the basis for why the women have come to call on the King of Kabul, but beyond that it has little to do with what actually happens. It is a difficult scene. We had worked on it almost every day since we had started rehearsing, it was always a mess.

Even after the actors began to understand their lines, they were not immediately aware that some of the lines were supposed to be funny. That took a few more weeks to become evident. One thing that did not make any sense to anybody was that two characters could speak to one another without the others overhearing. Nor did anyone have any sense of the importance of timing in the interplay between the servants acting as messengers between the nobles and ladies.

"No, you are supposed to leave the stage now," Corinne would say as she gently guided an actor out of the way. They would look at me with unhappy eyes that asked, "Why is she pushing me?" Pushing Afghans is an excellent way to start a fight. I would quickly explain what she was doing, but by the time I did, Corinne was already speaking to another actor, and I had to catch up on that conversation.

And then one day, after all the usual interruptions for arguments, urgent trips to the bathroom and tea, we ran the whole scene, and everyone did it perfectly. Corinne applauded, and the actors applauded themselves. Then we did it again, and it was even better. Suddenly, we had a scene. Characters had come alive. The action was crisp. Lines were spoken as if they were the actors' own words.

This was a breakthrough like no other. Corinne was joyful all the way home, and all that evening. Stephen was there, and we all sat up on the terrace of the old fort celebrating our great success. My mother cooked some special foods for us, including her aubergines sautéed in garlic butter, dribbled with yoghurt. We listened to the wind sift through the old tall trees that arched over the courtyard and the thick stand of lilac bushes at its centre. Finally, we were having some cooler air. Water gurgled in the eight-sided fountain. We were filled with a great sense of accomplishment.

∾

The next day when we arrived back at the Foundation, Corinne said, "Let's start by running that scene we all did so well yesterday." The actors all took their places.

"Let's start," Corinne said. "Enter Haroon, Sherzad, Mansour and Sohrab." No one moved. The actors appeared not to remember what they were supposed to do. They looked at one another, and looked at their scripts. Corinne looked like she wanted to cry, except that she is not a weeper. This time, her voice went up instead of down.

"How could you have forgotten everything?" she asked in total disbelief. I felt sorry for her. And for me, because this meant I now had to translate all the unhappy things she wanted the actors to hear, and then I would have to hear all the unhappy things that the actors did not want me to translate for her.

Instead of telling them exactly what Corinne was saying, I simply said to this one and that one, "Don't you remember that when he comes in, you are supposed to go over there and say that?"

Then they would look at me, and say, "Yes, Qais jan, I remember that. I can do that. But we did that yesterday. Why do we want to do it again?" I did my best to explain the idea of rehearsing. After a few minutes, the actors found their memories from the day before, and did the scene again, almost perfectly. We went on to the next scene.

∾

The one actor who had the most trouble remembering his lines and his cues was Kabir. He never seemed to know what to do. He was a very nice man. He was always the first actor to arrive. He would do anything that Corinne asked him to do. But he could never remember anything for long.

One day, I could see that Corinne was becoming exasperated with him, and understandably so. He kept stumbling over lines in scenes we had rehearsed several times. He was supposed to say:

SIKANDER
If my observation, which very seldom lies,
By the heart's still rhetoric disclosed with eyes,
Deceive me not now, the king is infected.

But it would come out as "his eyes are infected," or that "the king seldom lies." It was all a jumble.

I took him to one side during the tea break to explain to him that he really needed to try harder to remember things. Very gently, I said to him, "Kabir jan, when Corinne tells you to act like a messenger in a scene, you act like a king of old days. When she tells you to act like a funny man, you are too serious. When she tells you not to move your hands when you talk, you wave them all around. When she tells you to move your hands when you talk, you don't move them. This is a problem. Is there some way to fix it?"

He replied, "I don't know. Sometimes these things happen. They just do. I don't know how to stop them."

Then he told me some things about himself. He said, "During the fighting, I was beaten many times by different factions. Once I was on my way to our house. In our neighbourhood, the Uzbeks were in charge. From where I had come from my brother's house, Gulbuddin (a Pashtun) was in charge. They were both fighting against each other, sending countless rockets at each other. The Uzbeks thought I was a spy for Gulbuddin. They beat me on the head with the back of their guns, and punched me in the face. Then they kicked me all over my body while I lay crumpled on the floor. I kept shouting that I was not a spy. But they kept beating me.

"This same thing happened three or four times with other factions, always for the wrong reasons. I was only trying to take care of my family. As a result, now I can't easily memorise my lines, and I forget my moves. Some may think I'm not a good actor, but I used to be," he said very earnestly, as his voice caught. "I used to be a very good actor."

I told these things to Corinne on the way home that evening. She did not say anything. But from then on, she treated Kabir very kindly, and always helped him remember when he could not remember by himself. Slowly, his confidence started to grow, and he made fewer mistakes. Everyone else helped him as well, because he was the oldest person in our group and deserved our respect. And besides, everybody liked him, even though he said little, and rarely told jokes.

16

Exits and Entrances

Kabul. August, 2005.

One day during the fourth week of rehearsals, after yet another dispute with Corinne about some small thing, Nabi Tanha announced that he did not want to play his part unless he received more pay than the other actors.

"I have more lines and movements than everyone else, and I should be paid more than others," he told me. "If Corinne still wants me to play my part, I have to bring some changes into the text, and into all our movements. I will show them how to do it. Or at least Corinne has to ask me for my help. Everyone everywhere respects me, but she doesn't think of me even as a walnut."

Nabi Tanha was working himself up to a big scene. His back was straight. He stood like he was giving orders.

"Nothing is more important in the world to me than respect," he went on. "If someone respects me, then that is everything for me. But here she looks at me as she sees the others. I am totally different from the others. My education, my acting, my personality, my sense of humour, my theatre knowledge and so on. She has to notice all these, otherwise I will leave this project. If still she treats me like the others, and pays me only as much as the others, then she has to change my part with someone else and give me a smaller one."

I took a deep breath and started translating all these things to

Corinne, who then began shouting at me, though she was really shouting at Nabi Tanha.

Corinne said, "How dare you say such things! You can't leave the project. And you can't bring any changes into the text or the movements. I am the director, not you.

"I do respect you," she went on, "but you are no different from the others. We are all the same. I believe you are more educated than the others, but your education is not special. If you want me to change your part, I can do that. But you must learn it and stay with it from now on. You have to stand on your word.

"You were the one who said, 'If you were with us for six months we could challenge the whole country.' Now you want to challenge me. You want to be the director. You want to change the text. You want to do things that are not yours to do. But you're afraid of having so many lines. So, how would you do all these other things?"

Nabi Tanha drew himself up and spoke quietly with anger burning in his eyes. "Yes, you're absolutely right," he said, "and I am absolutely wrong! Now, I am leaving. You can cast someone else instead of me. Good luck! Goodbye!'

Corinne looked at him with her mouth open. "What?"

"I said I am leaving," Nabi Tanha repeated. "I don't want to be part of this project anymore."

"OK. No problem," Corinne replied.

"Once again," said Nabi Tanha who was milking the moment, "goodbye, and I shall never see you again." Nabi started to walk off the stage, and toward the door.

Sabah Sahar came over to Corinne and spoke to her quietly for a moment, saying she needed to go out for a few minutes. Corinne nodded distractedly. Sabah Sahar followed Nabi Tanha out the door.

All the other actors started chattering to one another. Corinne busied herself with the text. Every couple of minutes she asked me about things we did not need to talk about. She seemed a bit lost. She was probably asking herself, 'Who should I cast instead of Nabi Tanha?'

Nabi Tanha and Sabah Sahar came back.

Nabi Tanha pointed at Corinne and said, "I was leaving, but Sabah Sahar didn't let me. She said it is rude to leave like this. I just came back because of Sabah Sahar, not you."

Corinne looked at him like he was somebody she found annoying. "Then work for Sabah Sahar," she said. "Not for me. You're not part of my project anymore. I don't need you."

Nabi Tanha was now defiant. "No! I am gonna be in this play, and work for you, and you have to change my part."

"Are you commanding me," Corinne asked in disbelief, "or making a suggestion to me?"

Nabi Tanha turned stoic. "Whatever you think."

Corinne's father was a Kurd from Syria. Perhaps he had taught her the ways of the bazaar at an early age, or maybe they were just in her blood, but she knows the art of bargaining better than most. I had taken her to some carpet stores in Kabul a few times and watched as she haggled over the prices like an Afghan. She knew all the tricks. I could see her mind was moving in that direction now. She was looking to make a deal.

"I will change your part with Arif," she said.

Arif immediately interjected, politely, "That would be difficult for me. I have already memorised all my lines, and I have my exams at the university soon. I don't have time to memorise someone else's lines. We had to decide these things three weeks ago, not now. I am sorry, Nabi jan, you have to find a way to solve your problem, not me."

Arif was not part of Nabi Tanha's faction. Nabi Tanha could not tell him what to do. He dismissed Arif with a wave of his hand and said, "Fine. I am leaving. This is the last time I say this." Then he pointed to the other actors and said, "I warn you people, you won't achieve anything by doing this stupid project. You have to listen to me, otherwise you will regret this one day. You have to understand that this play will have repercussions. You will all become targets. It will become a threat to your life and your family. Goodbye!"

Corinne did not know what he said. I did not want to translate. Nabi Tanha picked up his bag and started to leave.

Corinne looked at him, "I thought you were coming back. Qais, what is happening? Is he coming back?" Nabi Tanha was by then out of the door. I simply said, "No."

Corinne shook her head and looked at the actors who were all very quiet. "Arif," she said, "you have to play Nabi Tanha's part. I will find someone else for your part."

Our first performance was in two weeks.

∾

The next several days were very difficult. We continued with our rehearsals. By the end of that week, we had blocked out about a third of the play. The actors were remembering most of their lines and movements, but Arif had to read Nabi Tanha's part from the script, and I read his.

Then Corinne started catching many kinds of sicknesses. The weather was getting even hotter, some days reaching 45 degrees Centigrade (110 degrees Fahrenheit). Everyone started coming late again, and getting impatient and smoking cigarettes in the middle of rehearsal. Every day, someone was having diarrhea again, including myself on three different days. The costumes were not ready, though the seamstresses were working hard. Not all the props had been sourced as yet. Someone always seemed to have something discouraging to say. We began to feel that the play was not going to happen.

Meanwhile, the Afghan and foreign media began coming to do interviews. The actors and actresses all said good things about the production and how happy they were to be doing the play, and working with Corinne, and experiencing Shakespeare.

Many of the journalists focused on Marina, since *Osama* had won a Golden Globe Award and she was the best known in the cast. They all wanted to hear again how she was discovered by the film's director begging in Kabul. They quoted her as saying, "I had never heard of Shakespeare before this play. But I like this story from the beginning to the end." Everyone smiled.

But beneath all those good words, there was a sense of despair that the journalists could not see.

Faisal, for instance, was always very self-conscious. He wanted to believe that he is a good actor, but admitted that he made many mistakes in rehearsals. Sometimes he worried that everyone was thinking poorly of him.

He often asked me, "What do you think about me, Qais? What do the others say about me?" I never was sure how to answer, but he kept asking me.

Whenever he had a haircut, he asked more than hundred people hundreds of times, "How do I look? Who do I look like? Am I looking handsome? Why I am not looking handsome? Tell me?"

But he usually laughed before I could say anything. He liked to laugh. And to recite poetry. He had memorised thousands of lines of poetry. But some days, he had trouble remembering his lines.

❧

Nabi Tanha came back on Saturday while we were in the middle of the rehearsal. Everyone stopped as he entered the garden. Corinne looked at him with surprise and asked a bit sarcastically, "Have you come to watch us?"

Nabi Tanha was unusually subdued. "No, no!" he said with surprise in his voice, "I have come back to join the play."

"That's interesting," Corinne said in a voice that made it clear that she did not find it interesting. But she had not been able to find an actor in the week that Nabi Tanha had been gone. Her bazaar haggling instincts swung into action. She said nothing else, and waited for Nabi Tanha to make the next move.

He put down his bag at the edge of the stage, as he climbed the three steps to join us.

"I needed the time to reflect. Now I regret my past actions," he said. "I shouldn't have behaved that way. I thought a lot about all of you this week. Finally, I found myself guilty. I tried hard not to come back, but my conscience didn't let me stay away any longer. In fact, my heart takes me everywhere, not my feet. I dreamt several times about our fighting. I saw both of us in my dream. I found myself stupid and foolish."

His usual lofty demeanour was nowhere to be seen that day.

"I know I was wrong," he went on. "Now I want to be part of this play. Or if you don't give me my part back, I will play any part you want me to. If you don't want me at all to be a member of this project, I will stay here until you give up, and give me a part to play. I don't care about my salary. Just show some respect. That is all. Not just towards me, but to everyone else. That is all."

Corinne spoke calmly. "I am glad you understand your mistakes. I don't want to talk about the past. Now if you want to be a member of this project, you have to play Arif's part."

Nabi Tanha brightened immediately. "That is great. I really appreciate it. I will do my best to bring happiness to you."

Sabah Sahar gave him one of her arch looks, and said teasingly, "I would be surprised if you mean that."

"You shouldn't put yourself in the middle of this," he snorted back. "It is none of your business."

Parwin begged to interrupt. "What about us? Are we none of your business, too?"

"Please don't start again," Nabi Tanha pleaded. "I just talked for all of you. The respect part. You also have to know that I have emotional problems sometimes. My brain doesn't work sometimes. It is all the result of the war. Then I think about my stupidity, and suffer for weeks. I don't want to talk about anything I did. Let me concentrate on my lines. I have a lot of work to do."

The rest of that day was a good day. Everybody worked hard. Nabi Tanha started joking with everyone to make them laugh. He also told everyone to concentrate on their movements and lines, to make Corinne happy. Suddenly, scenes that had always been a shambles started to flow.

Arif had already learned most of his new lines in the week Nabi Tanha was away. It was a challenge for Nabi Tanha to learn all of his new lines as fast as possible, and within days he was speaking without the script as well.

∾

The day after Nabi Tanha returned, a phone started to ring in the middle of rehearsal, even though Corinne had clearly instructed everyone to turn off their mobiles. It sounded extra loud because we were working inside that day.

"Whose phone is this?" Corinne asked sharply. "How many times should I tell you to please turn off your mobiles?"

Breshna Bahar had run to her large bag at the side of the room and was milling through it looking for the ringing phone. "Sorry, this is my phone. I have to answer it."

"No! We're not going to stop while you take a call," Corinne insisted. "I myself turn off my phone. How many times has it been said that we turn off our phones during the rehearsal? You have to know the rule!"

Breshna Bahar had located the phone and was raising it to her ear. "This will take only a moment," she said in English, "then I will respect the rule."

"No, No! You will respect the rule right now, this minute!" The anxieties of the past weeks and the looming date of the first performances all jumped into Corinne's face, and made her angrier than we had ever seen her.

Breshna Bahar shouted at her in Dari, "Shut up, you fool! Your rule is not God's rule! It is your rule, and I can break it." She looked at me, and asked me not to translate. I had to come up with something, as always. Then switching to English, she added. "This is my boss at the Ministry of the Interior. I must take his call." But by then the call had cut off by itself.

Breshna Bahar walked away from us saying, "Now I have to call him back." Everyone was looking at her as she punched in the number. She narrowed her eyes as she spoke with her boss. Her face became inflamed and red. She started shouting, "When did it happen? Where did it happen? Give me the address! Who's involved? Did you recognise any of them? Were they Pakistanis? Oh, no! How much were they carrying?"

We didn't know what she was talking about.

Corinne was all worked up by then. She did not need a sideshow by Breshna Bahar on top of everything else. "Enough! Enough!" she stated with her deepest and most authoritative voice. "We can't wait for you. Let's start." By then, Breshna Bahar was throwing her phone back into her bag, and was more worked up than Corinne.

"Do you know what happened?" she shouted in Dari. I groaned. What next, I thought? "Of course not! You just stand there yelling 'Enough! Enough!' while a gang of Pakistani criminals is trying to smuggle hashish and heroin from Afghanistan to Pakistan and then from Pakistan to Dubai. It is my job to arrest them." Then she added in English, "I have to go."

"Absolutely not!" Corinne stated indignantly, not having heard the rest. "You can't just leave in the middle of rehearsal. You were already

late coming today. You don't know your lines, your movements and
– "

Breshna Bahar looked at her like she was someone insignificant.
"Yes, I can leave now. I don't care for your rehearsal, your lines, your
movements…" she fumed as she zipped her bag. "I can't stay here and
let a bunch of stupid Pakistanis do their corruption in my country.
Enough! We are sick of this corruption in Afghanistan. We have to
stop them, and I am going to stop them now. I am leaving, and see
you tomorrow. Goodbye!"

She ran out the door, and was gone.

Corinne did not ask me to interpret. She just walked slowly out of
the room, and we did not see her again for more than an hour. Chat-
ters started among the actors.

One said, "She did what she had to do."

Another said, "I think she was right."

The next said, "She could have done it tomorrow."

A fourth said, "How could she do that tomorrow? Let them go to
Pakistan and arrest them there?"

Though it was early, we decided to go and have our tea, since we
did not know where Corinne had gone. And, of course, since Breshna
Bahar was not there, we all talked about her.

She had been more open with us about her life outside the play
than some of the others. She was in her late thirties. She had lost her
husband to an artillery round in 1992 during the civil war. Now she
was living with her mother and two daughters, all of whom she supported. In Taliban times, she had gone hungry. Now she was a policewoman, driving her own car. She had discovered that she could make
extra money by working in films. The pay was low, but she enjoyed
performing.

One time she told us, "I stepped into the world of movies after
the Taliban collapsed. First, I appeared in advertisements for companies selling things like washing machines, TVs, DVD players and so
on. This attracted the attention of some film companies. Then Nabi
Tanha asked me to be in his *Bulbul* movie, which made me famous.

"Now whenever I go out, people call me, 'Gul Chaira jan, how is
your husband Bulbul?' That makes me miss my own husband. Bulbul
was my husband only in the movie, and they know he is not my real

husband. I feel I am being insulted. But I smile, and say nothing. I smile in my face, and cry in my heart."

Ironically, with Nabi Tanha's change of roles in *Love's Labour's Lost*, he and Breshna Bahar were once again paired up. Many Afghans who came to see the play thought we had done that on purpose.

∾

Breshna Bahar came back two days later. Corinne did not say anything to her. In a real world, she would have been fired. But Corinne knew she could not find anyone else in so short a time. We had only a little more than one week left until the first performance. And so far, we had rehearsed less than half of the play. Things, though, were moving faster every day. The actors had finally begun to get a sense of what it was like to be on stage. They learned basic stage tricks, like how to speak to each other while also speaking to the audience.

The women were forgetting to be shy with the men. Now they were looking into each other's eyes when they spoke, and standing next to the men when they needed to. The good feelings had come back again, but one of the most difficult scenes lay ahead.

17

Expulsion of the Russians

Kabul. August, 2005.

We had reached the scene in which the boys were supposed to dress up like Russians. By then, the young nobles have confessed to each other that they are in love with the women and want to go see them, but they are ashamed to tell the women that they have decided to break their vow of celibacy. They come up with the idea that if they disguise themselves as Russians, the women will not recognise them. It was like something right out of a Bollywood movie.

When Corinne explained the scene to the actors, they all made sour faces. She asked them to start reading the lines, but nobody did.

Nabi Tanha, who despite everything still saw himself as the spokesman for the actors, looked at Corinne with disbelief in his eyes.

"Japan won its independence one day before us," he said. "Look where they are today, and where we are today. We are so backward, in the 13th century. Why? Because of politics. Who is responsible for our backwardness? England and Russia. The permanent wounds that the Russians left behind, in our hearts and in our souls, they're still fresh. Corinne, now you put salt on fresh wounds by telling us to disguise ourselves as Russians. How can you do this to us?"

Corinne was taken aback. She did not know what to say. She looked around at the other men. Shah Mohammed added, "I do not think we should be Russians." Faisal nodded his head in agreement, and Arif said, "I agree with them. We cannot be Russians."

The girls were nodding as well. Corinne looked at me. I had an idea.

"What about Indians?" I asked. I started saying a few things about Afghans, and what makes them laugh, and how we could do this by changing the Russians to Indians.

All the actors looked at me, and slowly the grim looks on their faces were conquered by intrigued smiles as the idea played in their minds. Corinne did not say "No," as I had expected, but she did not like the idea. She had been very sick that day, and was tired. It was near the end of the day.

I said, "Corinne, go home and relax. We will change the Russian part to an Indian part. That is how we will do it." She left looking discouraged, and without saying goodbye. She did not even call me from the car, which she always did on the other days when she had left early.

Now I had to come up with something. Like Corinne, I asked all the actors to sit in a big circle. I took my notebook and pen, and asked each one of them if they had any ideas to help me do this scene. I had never talked to them in that way. It was not my position to tell them what to do, since I was younger than all of them except for Marina and Leila. But that day, they listened to me carefully and understood my concerns.

One actor suggested an Indian song, another suggested Bollywood dancing, another suggested Gandhi clothes, another suggest Indian turbans, another suggested the red dot on the forehead, another suggested Indian royal slippers.

Their suggestions sounded great to me. "All we are missing is the script," I told them. "Let's do an improvisation," I suggested.

Before they started, I looked around and found a few Afghans who were at the Foundation that afternoon, and asked them to be our audience. I gave each of them a pen and paper, and asked them to jot down their reactions to the scene we were going to improvise.

The actors started. They each sang a Bollywood song, and danced. They were hilarious, but they did not know what to say when they had finished singing. One of them told a joke in Urdu that made everyone laugh. Nearly everyone in Afghanistan understands Urdu. We watch hundreds of Bollywood movies every year. The Hindi they speak in the movies is more or less the same as Urdu, except written in a different alphabet. Many Afghans speak Urdu well, especially those who once lived in Pakistan as refugees. This gave me an idea.

I collected the papers from the audience. Some wrote only one line, while others filled the whole page, back and front. I dismissed the cast and promised them a script by the next day. I asked them to come one hour early to work on what I planned to write overnight.

I worked late, writing jokes, discarding them, writing more until I had a scene – in Urdu.

The next day, they all showed up early, as I had requested. Corinne was not yet at the Foundation. I led the actors in some vocal exercises the way she always did, then gave the boys the script, and walked them through it a couple of times. Like Dari, Urdu is written with the Arabic alphabet, so it was easy for all the guys to read. We made a few changes until everyone was happy with it.

When Corinne came, I said to her, "Let the actors do some Indian improvisations we created last night."

First, she said "No," but that day I was not accepting "No." I simply told her very politely that the actors were going to do the scene, then asked them to take their positions. She said, "Go ahead, then. Quickly, because we don't have much time." She slumped onto a chair, still drained by her sickness from the day before.

The actors began. When they spoke the words I had written, the lines became even funnier than when I had heard them in my head. From the very beginning, Corinne sat up. Her exhaustion disappeared from her face as she started laughing. She laughed so hard that at first she became red, and then blue, even though she had no idea what the actors were saying. She just could not stop laughing.

The sound of our laughter brought some of the employees of the Foundation who were curious to see what was going on. The actors were energised by having an audience that kept growing as more employees arrived. The audience also laughed loudly and demanded to see the scene again. We did it, and everyone laughed even more than before.

Corinne said, "Qais, great job! We don't need to work on this scene again. Let's focus on the other scenes."

Later that day, we did the Indian scene again. By then Qaseem

Elmi had arrived. He had been coming to rehearsals for the past week or so, amazed to see that the script, which had been such a burden for him, was filled with so much life. He had never seen a play before, and was astonished at the level of intensity that came from having actors performing in front of him, and not just speaking from a screen.

He and Stephen had come with Ali Khan. They needed to get information from the actors for a programme booklet they were preparing in English and Dari. Ali Khan had become good friends with Daoud. They shared a sense of humour, and often sat to one side telling jokes.

We started doing the Indian scene. Everybody who had seen us in the morning had told all the others who worked in the Foundation about it. When they saw us doing it again, they rushed out of their offices and into the garden. As soon as Nabi Tanha began his song, they started laughing. By the time he had finished, the laughter had become a roar.

Daoud was clapping in time to the music, as were many others. Qaseem was holding his hands wide apart in the air and moving his shoulders as if he were dancing *bhangra*. Ali Khan was shouting "Yes! Yes! Yes!" And Stephen was thrilled: Bollywood was back in the script.

∼

That same day the costumes arrived. They were so beautiful, both the boys' and the girls'. Shahla Nawabi brought one of her seamstresses with her and made a few adjustments on the girls' costumes. But everything fit well and made everyone look royal.

The next day, we had a dress rehearsal. The stage at the end of the garden had been removed overnight to make room for the chairs for our audience. We held the dress rehearsal on the grass in the centre of the garden, exactly the same place where we had all sat on the Hazaragi *kilim* five months before and talked about doing a play.

Rahim Walizada's beautiful carpets had arrived, and they now covered the wooden platform, making it look very kingly.

For a first full run-through, it was not bad, but Corinne was not happy with it. Some of the actors forgot to come on stage when they were supposed to. Others messed up their lines in a few places. By now Corinne had heard the lines so often that, even though she did not speak Dari, she could tell if the actors were saying what they were supposed to be saying.

Now, we had one day left before the first performance. The next afternoon, the actors went first to the salon, sat in a large circle and read through the script together. Afterwards, we did another run-through in the garden. It was one of those days when nobody seemed to know what to do. There were long waits for actors who forgot to come on. Props could not be found.

Our first performance was the next day. We were not ready, but what could we do? The Foundation had already sent out invitation cards.

Resolution

by Qais Akbar Omar
and
Stephen Landrigan

18

Performance

Kabul. August 31, 2005.

Opening night. For the first time, all of the actors arrived at the Foundation on time. They put on their costumes very quietly. They all used one dressing room. The men went in first, and when they were finished, the women used it. We had come a long way from the days when the girls would not look at the boys. They had decided themselves that they all wanted to be together in one room.

Nobody wasted time chatting, or using the bathroom, or drinking tea, or eating, or smoking, or arguing about silly issues. Everybody had a script and was going over lines. They all looked nervous.

The garden of the Foundation filled up as soon as the doors opened. Foreigners were offered the seats in the first row. Among them was Malcolm Jardine, along with several of his colleagues from the British Council. Malcolm was beaming like a proud uncle.

Afghans filled the other seats, all talking to one another. About a hundred chairs had been set out in a semi-circle around the playing area. Within minutes, they were filled.

Mustafa Haidari, who worked at the Foundation, was the man who always solved our problems. Anything we needed, Mustafa would make it appear or happen. Now he was racing around with other Foundation staff locating additional chairs as people continued to pour in.

With all the seats filled, some of the new arrivals settled on the carpets in the playing area, not understanding that this was where the actors would be appearing shortly. One man tried to set a chair between the *takht* of the King of Kabul and the tent of the Princess of Herat.

The ever-increasing audience was the kind of problem that any theatre impresario anywhere could only dream about.

In the end, we never really knew how many we had in the audience. Estimates that appeared in the media in the days that followed varied. One suggested four hundred, others less. We had no way to get an exact count. But the garden was densely packed with people, and the excitement that they generated was intense.

The time to begin was approaching. Corinne had joined the actors and the rest of the company in a room at the edge of the garden. She was dressed in a beautiful ankle-length Afghan dress that was covered with elaborate embroidery. With her dark hair and eyes, she could easily have been taken as an Afghan woman.

She asked that everyone hold hands, close their eyes and take a deep breath. We did. She said, "Open your eyes." We did. Then she said, "Everybody say '*Merde!*' in one loud voice." We did, even though we did not know what it meant.

"What is '*Merde*'?" Nabi Tanha asked.

She smiled, and said, "It is French. It means 'shit.'"

"So, we are now supposed to do a shitty performance?" Nabi Tanha asked incredulously.

"No, no, it is just a French tradition," Corinne reassured him. "We always say it before a performance."

"A weird tradition!" the actors exclaimed, in a rare moment of total agreement.

The boys left to take their positions on the other side of the stage. They waited for the play to begin in a garden shed out of the sight of the audience. The clock struck 5:00pm. Time to start.

The King and his nobles made their first appearance. As they entered, the audience immediately quieted, but a donkey outside the Foundation started braying so loudly that we could hardly hear Shah Mohammed as he spoke his opening lines. The audience broke out into big laughs as he tried to out-shout the donkey. The other actors forced their jaws into a locked position, and kept their own laughs inside.

Finally, the donkey stopped, and Shah Mohammed looked triumphant, as if he had won a competition. Nabi Tanha, now as Sherzad, was the second actor to speak. A low rumble of approval rose from the Afghans as he took centre stage. "Wah, wah, wah, wah, wah…." Here they were seeing 'Bulbul' in real life, and that made them happy.

∽

The first joke comes about two minutes into the script when Sohrab, played now by Arif, suddenly realises that the vow he has casually made to study for three years with the King also includes a provision that he cannot talk with women for all that time. Somehow, Sohrab had missed that point.

The look on Arif's face as he digested this unexpected news sent a wave of tentative laughter through the Afghans. They seemed undecided on whether they were meant to laugh out loud. But from that moment, they understood that the show was going to be funny.

The foreigners, not understanding Dari, had no idea what Arif had said. But they could tell from his face that it had been something humourous. They responded with the smiles of polite guests showing approval.

A few minutes later, the girls entered. A buzz went through the crowd. History was being made as women and men stood together on a stage. For the Afghan men in the audience, especially the younger ones, seeing women like this was a rare experience, and something close to a thrill.

The audience, though, was also reacting to the girls' costumes, which looked rich and regal in the early evening light. The girls walked with dignity and grace as the swirls of fabric wafted around them. Shahla Nawabi sat to one side scrutinising the costumes, and nodding in approval.

Sabah Sahar led the girls in a stately pace, her artfully applied make-up completely intact, as she had always said it would be.

For those of us who had seen the production take shape, and been aware of the sometimes fractious rehearsals, nothing surprised us more than seeing Breshna Bahar moving with feminine airs and graces she had never before revealed. She was every inch a noble-woman, with her tough policewoman's persona nowhere to be seen. The delicate way that she moved her hands, the shyness with which she smiled, the overall sweetness that she projected through her character were utterly unexpected. She had kept her mastery of the craft of acting as much a secret as her detective work.

But no one in the cast was more transformed than Marina. Where was the giggling, frightened girl who had choked on her lines in rehearsal? Who was this woman who spoke with the sophistication of someone ten years older than Marina? Who moved with total assurance. Who could dismiss a riposte from Arif as Sohrab with a killer glance. Who could exchange badinage with the other actors as if she were born speaking in witty epigrams. Was this our little Marina? We were stunned, and entranced. As the performance progressed, she seemed to grow into the role, exuding the self-confidence bordering on hauteur that Shakespeare had intended.

The first moments the women are on stage are very formal, as the Princess of Herat explains her mission. She has come to settle an old financial dispute between her father in Herat and the King of Kabul. While that is going on, the men try hard not to reveal their immediate interest in the women.

The verbal interplay between the King and the Princess went smoothly, with more quiet ripples of Afghan laughter, especially as the women accompanying the Princess confided their opinions of the men to one another. Then the banter between the men and women began with Arif as Sohrab addressing Marina as Senober.

SOHRAB
Did not I see you dance in Kunduz once?

SENOBER
Did not I see you *dance in Kunduz once?*

SOHRAB
I know I did.

SENOBER
How needless was it then to ask the question!

The Afghan laughter was becoming more confident, more robust. Perhaps it was the inclusion of a reference to the northern Afghan city of Kunduz. Perhaps it was the unexpected snap-back from Marina to Arif's question. By the next scene, Sohrab is already trying to set up a secret rendezvous with Senober with the help of Parwin's character, Fatima. The audience was eagerly waiting for the next funny line.

As the madcap efforts of the men to communicate with the women unobserved mounted, the shyness in the audience eased. At one point, Arif sought a hiding place by climbing a tree. Nabi Tanha, in turn, took refuge behind the same tree. Faisal ran around like a cat being chased by a dog, and ended up under the same tree. Though he pulled a branch to cover his face, the rest of his body was plainly visible. And Shah Mohammed's serious-minded King of Kabul, when caught with amorous intentions of his own, first looked to his right and then to his left, then raced towards a flight of stairs.

Once the men discover each other's schemes and decide to pursue the women, the King of Kabul gives the battle cry: "Soldiers to the field!" Big laugh.

While the laughs were one way to track the audience's interest, a look at their faces showed how intently they were engrossed in this story as it was unfolding. They all gave the appearance of being totally engaged, even the foreigners. We had given them a printed programme that included scene-by-scene synopsis in English. Many of them told us later that while the synopsis was welcome, they had no trouble following the story, because of the clarity of the acting.

∾

The show continued smoothly. The actors made not even one mistake. Not one line was forgotten, which had been our biggest concern. Neither Kabir nor Parwin showed any hesitation or difficulty in remembering anything. Later, both said that running the entire show straight through had made things easier for them, instead of doing only a scene at a time, as in rehearsals.

The only distractions came from a few ringing mobile phones in the audience, the honking of the cars and buses from outside, the noise of military helicopters passing overhead, and a child who wandered across the stage.

Midway through the performance, a nearby mosque called for evening prayers at sunset. A small number of men in the audience got up from where they were sitting. They went to the far side of the courtyard to an open area behind some tall rose bushes where we had not put seats, as the view from there to the playing area was blocked. The men laid their head scarves out on the stone pavement, said their evening prayers, then headed back to their seats.

This created a little problem as some of them came back through the playing area and climbed over the foreigners in the first row and the Afghans who had not prayed. When they got back to their seats, a few found that their seats had been taken by those who had been standing in the rear. The praying men whispered to the seat-grabbing guys in a threatening tone and demanded that the new arrivals get up. We tried to hush them. Some accepted our pleas, and went elsewhere. Others stared at us with drawn foreheads and narrowing eyes, and insisted on having their seats back.

With the sun gone, the floodlights we had set up around the garden began to add a different quality to the fabrics in the costumes. Shahla Nawabi had chosen them well. What had been eye-filling in the daylight became visually sumptuous under the lights.

Meanwhile, the kerosene lamps in the houses on the small mountain behind the Foundation were being lit. Their soft light filled the windows of countless mud-brick houses that perch in rows up the mountain. Youngsters were standing on their roofs, looking down into the Foundation's garden, trying to see what was going on. A couple of boys were flying kites over our heads. The kids slowly disappeared as the darkness deepened, but the lights in the houses twinkled like stars.

∽

Now we had reached the scene when the men come on as Indians, shirtless and wearing only *dhotis*, long panels of white cotton cloth wrapped around their waists with the end pulled through their legs. They had dots on their foreheads, for which they planned to use the girls' lipstick. Backstage, the boys had had to search all the actresses' bags for lipstick. We had forgotten to arrange that. Finally, Nabi Tanha found one in Breshna Bahar's bag, and exclaimed, "Here it is!" A sparkle appeared on all the boys' faces as if they had retrieved the Koh-e-Noor diamond.

Nabi Tanha was the first to enter. The audience had not expected anything like this. Laughter erupted that only grew as Nabi Tanha started singing a well-known Bollywood song that everybody had heard for years, *Hey Ninee Gori, Hey Ninee Gori*.

No sooner had he finished, than Faisal followed by Shah Mohammed and then Arif appeared in turn, singing equally well-known tunes. Arif is an excellent actor, but as the others joked about him in the Afghan way, he does not have an ant's talent as a singer. That only made his song funnier. Everybody laughed at him more than the other boys for how he tortured a song that even babies can sing, as Afghans say.

The audience were out of their seats clapping, cheering, screaming with laughter. The sudden switch to Urdu had brought it all home. The Afghans no longer felt they had to be polite; they were having too much fun. The play was now about them. Not about Shakespeare. Not about kings. Not about princesses. Not about Taliban rules. This was the new Afghanistan, and it was happening right there in front of them, as comically clad men sang outrageously funny songs to women seated with them on a stage, laughing themselves silly.

And the foreigners, though most of them probably did not know Urdu any more than they knew Dari, could not help but be caught up in the wildly joyous excitement all around them. They clapped and cheered with everyone else. The ten minutes or so that it took to play that scene was a living definition of euphoria.

We stood at the back, bent over with laughter, trying hard to not miss a moment. The uproarious audience approval was beyond anything we had expected. When the scene finally ended, we looked at Corinne, who had been laughing as hard as everyone else. She looked at us, and raised her eyebrows, which meant, "Good job!"

For reasons we did not know, Faisal had come on in that scene wearing a black T-shirt along with his *dhoti*. He wore the shirt inside out, but it was still possible to read the words "Pizza Hut" in reverse. It looked awful. Someone in the audience jokingly shouted in boisterous Afghan style, "Where is your tray of pizza?" It brought an extra laugh, but not one we really wanted.

After the show, Faisal told us that he did not want the audience to see the large, ugly scars that he bore from the shrapnel wounds he had suffered on the night his five friends were killed. He wanted to be handsome. Understood. So, for the remaining performances, we found a way to tie his *dhoti* around his neck so that it not only covered the scars, but made his character look even funnier.

Now the actors could do no wrong. In a scene that followed, the boys chased the girls around the garden, and the audience went wild again. Before it was over four noble couples were poised to become four pairs of lovers. Actually, there were five couples. Parwin's Fatima and Kabir's Sikander appeared to have developed an interest in each other. Though both are middle-aged, they had begun to act like teenagers, giving hints with their eyes of their growing interest in each other. That made everybody laugh.

∽

The same Mustafa Haidari who solved all our problems now entered the play briefly to resolve the problem of the vow taken by the four young nobles. Looking severe and handsome as a Messenger from Herat, he arrived unexpectedly and ominously to announce that the father of the Princess has died. The women must return home.

The sudden somber moment, so typical of Indian movies, provided a gentle transition out of the hijinks of the previous scenes and led to the parting of the couples as they agree to meet again after one year.

In the meantime, the women set tasks for the men. Senober, for instance, demands that Sohrab take his wit to hospitals to cheer the sick, much to Sohrab's dismay.

Sabah Sahar's Princess was never more riveting to watch than in her last scene as she dictates terms to the men. The smitten King of Kabul begs her to accept him.

HAROON, KING OF KABUL
Now, at the latest minute of the hour,
Grant us your loves.

PRINCESS OF HERAT
A time, methinks, too short
To make a world-without-end bargain in.

Her self-assured presence allows no arguments. Several Afghan women in the audience could be seen to be smiling and nodding approval. As she prepares to leave, the Princess briefly takes the King's hand in hers. It was the first and only time that a man and a woman touched during the play. She initiates the action. It is unforced, and, in the end, unremarkable, because the actors have prepared the way for this moment so well. But with that touch, one more small piece of Afghan history was made.

A moment later, the Princess offers one of the best-known exit lines in all of Shakespeare.

PRINCESS OF HERAT
So now, you that way: we this way.

With wistful looks at the men, the women gathered up their skirts, and strolled out of the King's garden, leaving dented hearts full of promises and expectations. The audience did not wait for them to leave. They jumped to their feet, clapping, cheering, shouting.

The boys tried to make their exit as directed on the other side of the stage, but the audience surrounded them.

Both the boys and the girls returned to the stage. After bowing for several minutes, they sat down on the carpet-covered *takht* platform. Nabi Tanha started playing the harmonium and singing a famous Afghan folk song. Everyone in the cast joined him, as they swayed from side to side. Many in the audience sang along. The moment had been unplanned, and was all the more powerful because of that.

∽

More bows, more applause, and the actors ran off to their dressing room in the Foundation's old mansion. Before long, however, they were back in the garden greeting friends and relatives. The girls still wore their costumes, because everybody wanted to take photos with them in their beautiful outfits.

Marina, who on so many days during rehearsals had never been far from a giggle, stood very solemnly as several young men asked to have their photos taken with her. Their requests were very formal; her response was pure *noblesse oblige* as she allowed them to stand next to her while somebody focused and snapped. All those appearances at film festivals had taught her how to maintain her composure while being admired and ogled.

As soon as the cameras had been put away, though, and the eager young men had left, she smiled again. It would not have looked decent for a young Afghan woman to be seen smiling in a photograph with men she does not know. Some boundaries had been crossed that night; others remained in place.

Parwin's husband was smiling proudly at his wife's success. Dressed in a light-coloured western-style suit, he stood politely to one side while Parwin and the other actors received the plaudits of the audience. Their son and daughter stood next to him, as enthralled as he was. Members of the cast figured out who he was because of the two kids, who had become the mascots of the production. It was the first time that any of the actors had met him. The cast members introduced themselves, and congratulated him for Parwin's performance.

As the crowd thinned, the cast and their relatives moved into one of the rooms of the mansion where food had been set out on a long cloth laid on the floor, and Afghan *rabab* music was spreading its twangy joy from a CD player. Everyone settled themselves on *toshaks* as they ate and talked about the evening.

Nabi Tanha had a look of contentment that we did not often see from him. Lest anyone dare to offer any criticism, he noted, "Of course, we were concerned about the reaction of the audience, because you never know who they are – educated people or fundamentalists. It seems we had a nice group of educated people. But what is there to criticise?" he asked.

"We observed both our Afghan customs and Islamic Sharia. Still," he added with a trace of worry, "we have to be concerned with our next performances. Even if we have only one fundamentalist in the audience, it takes only one bomb to blow everybody up."

Shah Mohammed added, "If we had done pure Shakespeare in English, even the educated ones would have criticised us, because pure Shakespeare means imposing foreign culture on this country. We domesticated Shakespeare, and included Afghan music and jokes, which made the play look like an Afghan party."

As one of the Foundation staff nimbly stepped over the platters of food to pour tea, Sabah Sahar agreed, saying, "The tradition of theatre in Afghanistan is not as old as in the European countries. What is theatre? It means to express the joys and sorrows of a society in a poetic way.

"If we had the tradition of theatre in the way that the Europeans do," she continued, "then Rumi, Hafiz, Sa'di, Ba'del, Ja'mi, and all our other poets could have written plays as meaningful as Shakespeare's. Though our poets and Shakespeare lived in different centuries, they share the same insights about the human heart and soul."

∽

That night, the Afghan television networks like TOLO TV and Afghan National Television talked about the play during and after the evening news. That made many people curious about what we were doing. The next evening, we had nearly a thousand people in the street wanting to be in the audience. Though the Foundation had greatly increased the number of seats from the night before, there were still not nearly enough.

Corinne was concerned that a riot outside the gate could cause problems for the actors. She went to the entrance, and tried to stop the incoming flow. "Tell them they cannot come in," she told the door-keeper in her most commanding voice. "We have no seats left. We are full. Tell them to please come back tomorrow night," she implored.

The doorkeeper, a pleasant middle-aged man, smiled, but people kept pushing past him, with a couple of hundred more well-dressed Afghans, both men and women, still in the street trying to get in.

Finally, the thick wooden door to the Foundation was eased shut, to shouts of disapproval from those outside. They continued to mill around for some time, though, expecting that the doors would open after a while and let more in. We were very unhappy that we did not have room for all of them.

∼

At the first performance, most of the Afghans in the audience were men. When they saw that there was nothing anti-Islamic or un-Islamic in the play, they came back on subsequent evenings and brought their wives and daughters to see it.

Just before the third performance was to begin, several women in *burqas* led by a young man entered the garden. They made their way down the grand stairway that leads from the entrance to the grass, then found a place to sit in a far corner. They sat there quietly, pulling the *burqas* away from their faces whenever Marina came on stage. They hung on her every word. Their eyes filled with laughter at her many jokes, but they never made a sound. They looked at each other and shared their joy, but only among themselves.

They were Marina's mother and sisters, led by one of her brothers. Their pride in Marina was plainly evident, but as soon as the performance ended, they glided back up the grand staircase, and out the door.

19

The Queen's Palace

Kabul. September 4, 2005.

The job of bringing *Love's Labour's Lost* from the Foundation to the Bagh-e-Babur on the day of our performance there started early. Mustafa Haidari, the smiling solver of all problems, spent the morning with his team of workers moving the props, the costumes, the wooden platform, and the carpets, as well as all the chairs from the Foundation. He gave orders with sweet words and made his crew happy to be working with him.

In a country where men embrace when they meet, Mustafa is a champion hugger. By the way in which he greeted us just outside the marble-faced entrance of the Queen's Palace, we could see he was very excited. He grabbed our hands and led us through the covered passageway, bubbling with the anticipation of sharing something he had only himself that day discovered. Few Afghans have ever been inside the Queen's Palace.

He led us out onto the terrace that overlooks the garden. Now it was our turn to be excited. In the couple of weeks since we had last been there, the garden and the buildings around it had been utterly transformed by Jolyon Leslie's workers. Gone were the piles of rubble, the ladders and the buckets of stucco mud. Long sheets of burlap had been spread over the wet stucco on the walls so that it would dry evenly. More burlap hung between the arches, giving a tattered grandeur to the ruins.

The Queen's Palace lacked the well-tended grass of the Foundation's garden. Yet an attractive performing area had been created by laying four very large Hazaragi *kilims* in the dust in front of the terrace battlements. One of them was the same *kilim* on which we had sat during our first workshop, and which we had used so many times since.

Two of the other *kilims* were from the old fort where we were living. We had laid them out on our roof terrace there a couple of times for parties. They must have been full of dust, but they were only going to get more of it here. Who knows where the fourth one came from.

Most astonishingly, the remains of the old fountain that had appeared so ugly on our first visit had entirely vanished. Jolyon had said it would. And it had. Where the fountain had been, there were now many rows of white chairs set in a wide arc around the playing area. To one side, Hashmat Ghani's six-sided tent stood as a tantalising indication that something wonderful was going to happen.

At a quick look, it seemed as if there were at least twice as many chairs as had been used at the Foundation. In front of the first row of chairs was a line of *toshaks* laid out on the earth for those more comfortable sitting with their legs crossed on the ground. Mustafa proudly stated that, yes, there were more chairs, and even more were being brought from chair rental companies who usually provided them for weddings.

No tickets had been distributed, so no one had any idea who might show up, or how many. Several diplomats and other notables had accepted Malcolm Jardine's invitation to attend a reception hosted by the British Council following the performance. This was to be the British Council's first large public event in Kabul. Malcolm had organised the details with great care and anticipation. The unrestrained enthusiasm in the Afghan media that had heralded the first performance four evenings before, along with the growing international coverage that had followed, made it clear that this would be an event not to be missed.

∿

The actors arrived by midday. They needed to work with Corinne to adapt their blocking to this entirely new setting. The garden at the Foundation was small, with many places for the actors to hide behind bushes or in small rooms nearby and be out of sight when they were not on stage. At the Queen's Palace, everything was exposed. There was no tree for Sohrab to climb.

Despite the heat, the actors worked hard to solve the problems the new space presented. The success of the four performances at the Foundation had melded them into a company. They were living up to Nabi Tanha's boast back in April, "We could challenge the whole country."

Entrances were arranged. The boys would enter down the grand staircase stage right of the battlements. In their turn, the girls would descend the stairs stage left. This meant that the boys had to be in position and out of sight in one of the rooms still under construction before the doors were opened to let in the audience.

It was the kind of issue that might have brought fevered argument a few weeks earlier. Today, they all readily agreed to everything. There were no clearly marked walkways in the garden as there were at the Foundation on which the boys could chase the girls. Routes had to be fixed around the white chairs, and timings worked out for each couple to do their chase, and get back to the playing area.

We walked down one of the staircases that flanked the playing area to chat with some of the actors below. There is something about descending such stairs that causes one to walk with a bit more poise.

The King's platform was angled to one side of the *kilims* in the playing area. Its bare wood was a glaring contrast to the kaleidoscopic colours of the *kilims*. It needed some of Rahim Walizada's carpets that had covered it at the Foundation. Mustafa assured us that they had been brought from the Foundation. We went to look for them.

Several of the actors were hanging around outside the door leading into the ornate *hamam* chambers, which were being used as dressing rooms. Their welcomes were loud and exuberant. "My best friend!" Faisal exploded, exhausting his English vocabulary. Hugs all around.

Large trays of food for the actors' lunch had arrived just before we did. Nabi Tanha insisted we eat something, as every Afghan will do, even if he has only a single piece of bread to share. Inside, some of the girls were seated in a circle on the floor dishing out *pelau* and *kebab*, the mainstays of every Afghan picnic.

The atmosphere was electric. These actors were ready. It would be three hours before they finally marched out onto the stage, but the anticipation that they were generating was palpable. All the costumes were hanging neatly on a rack.

When everyone had had enough to eat, the singing started, then the dancing. The girls went to the next room, out of sight of the men, and whooped and laughed as they stretched out their arms in the sinuous moves and tiny steps that the women in their families had been doing for centuries.

And if some of the men happened to catch sight through the open door, well, they were all a kind of family now. No one would have defended the honour of those actresses more vigourously than the actors.

Perhaps the actors still did not absolutely understand everything that Shakespeare had written about love in the lines they spoke in the play, but, drawing on their own customs, they had crafted their own way of acknowledging their affection for one another while respecting the boundaries. If Corinne had achieved nothing else with this production, she had done that.

Rahim's carpets were carefully stacked in a corner on a blue UN tarp to keep them clean. Later, we carried several of them down to the playing area, and spread them over the bare wood of the platform. Immediately, it became as regal as its setting.

∾

Now it was a matter of waiting. It was a perfect time to take a walk around Babur's magnificent garden. Daoud came with us.

Though Daoud has the good looks of a Bollywood movie star, he could never pass a screen test. He freezes when a camera is pointed at him. He is by nature an entertainer, but not one who sets himself in front of others and seeks their applause. He is more subtle. He unobtrusively positions himself amid his audience, and gets them to be part of whatever song he is singing, or dance he is leading.

Daoud explained that this was the first time he had walked around the Bagh-e-Babur since he had been a little kid. By then in his early thirties, he was always filled with a young man's enthusiasm for anything new he encountered. And that day, he saw Babur's pool for the first time.

Maybe it was actually Abdur Rahman's pool. Some king had built it. Daoud was going to be in it. It was twice the size of an Olympic pool, with steps leading down the slope of the hill into its dark water. Daoud had no interest in the steps.

Though modesty is a deeply ingrained characteristic of Afghan people, even between husbands and wives, the sight of the water freed Daoud from all inhibitions. He rapidly pulled off his knee-length *kameez* shirt, and undid the knotted belt that held up his *shalwar* trousers. He stepped out of his sandals as the *shalwar* fell down around his ankles in a pair of crumpled cotton rings.

Wearing only his blue boxer shorts, he spread his arms towards the water, as if offering it a hug, laughed, and then made a perfect dive into its dust-clouded depths.

Few Afghans had ever had a chance to learn to swim in their arid country. Some may have gone to the manmade Qargha Lake just outside Kabul, or taken a dip in the stunningly azure lakes of Band-e-Amir in central Afghanistan, but most had not. The large municipal swimming pools built by the Communist government had not held water for nearly a generation.

Yet there was Daoud, when he finally resurfaced, executing all kinds of strokes, with his ever-luminescent smile.

The first night we had come to the Bagh-e-Babur, Jolyon told us that his team had put the word out to the workmen and the kids in the neighbourhood that the pool was full of snakes. It was not actually true. They were just trying to keep kids who could not swim from drowning. We did not have a chance to tell Daoud, and he probably would not have cared.

"Take a picture," shouted this most camera-shy of Afghans. We did. Several, in fact, as it quickly became evident that this was going to be a moment he would remember long after everything else that had happened during his brush with Shakespeare had begun to fade.

∾

We still had one hour before the performance.

The girls were putting on their make-up, joking and drinking tea. The boys were still making music as they began gathering up their costumes.

Corinne was talking animatedly to photographer Kate Brooks, who was snapping away, sometimes posing the performers, sometimes catching them unaware. Her photos would find their way into newspapers and magazines around the world in the days ahead, as did other photos made by Tomás Munita from the Associated Press, who arrived shortly after.

Marina was putting on her make-up. Kate Brooks snapped a photo of her that showed her as a poised, sophisticated young woman. From one performance to the next, Marina was finding new depth in her role as Senober. She finally understood what it meant to do theatre. The lines that had once so terrified her, now propelled her into an immediate rapport with her audience.

Faisal was already in his costume. He was always the first one to do so. As soon as he had, he would pick up his script and hold it in his hand as if it were part of his outfit. He would read his lines over and over, along with everyone else's.

From time to time, Faisal would join the boys, and sing with them. Daoud, now back in the *hamam*, would cheer him on. Faisal is a good singer. He called himself the Ahmad Zahir of the cast, after Afghanistan's best-known pop singer. But after one song, he would continue his rounds, as he did before every performance, to see what everybody was doing. He teased the girls for a few minutes. Then he came into the innermost room of the *hamam* complex.

"Qais jan, are you asleep?" he asked in a whispery voice.

I had stretched out on the cool marble floor to have a short rest alone, far from the actors. I opened my eyes a little, and looked up at him, "What is it, Faisal jan?" He came and stood over me.

"I have been reading the whole script in the past few days, many times," he said.

"That's good. Perhaps you can tell me more about it later," I said drowsily.

"I will, because the more I read it, the more it charms me." He sat down next to me. "I had no idea how deep this play is when I first read the script. It is like Rumi and Hafiz; it works on you later, after you digest it." He was talking very softly, as if he were worried he would wake someone. But I was the only one who had been sleeping.

"Did it take you so long to digest it?" I asked, hoping a joke would send him away. "What would you do if you had eaten old camel meat?"

"No, no, I'm serious!" Faisal's voice was making hoarse echoes in the domed white room. He leaned closer to me. "I really feel these words now as I say them. I really feel them. I have never read such a powerful script before. I don't think everybody in the group really understands the deepest meanings of these lines. I think they just say the words, because we are actors, and this is what we do. But now I really know what they mean."

"This is good to hear," I said to him as I yawned. "But please let me rest for a while. I'm very tired. I had to help arrange the chairs in the heat, and set up the stage and the tent, and I worked with you guys for a couple of hours. I will have a lot to do after half an hour. We will talk about all this another time."

"Okay, okay. Have your rest," Faisal whispered, and got up to leave.

"I am very happy for you that you have discovered these things, Faisal jan," I told him as he tiptoed out of the room.

"Thanks, Qais jan." Then, just as he was going through the arched door, he turned to me and said quietly, "I have heard that many Afghans have gone to live in England. Maybe Shakespeare was one of them."

❧

It was nearly time to start. The boys were checking their costumes. The girls were having last looks in the mirror for their make-up. Breshna Bahar handed her lipstick to Nabi Tanha so nobody would have to go looking for it when they came to the Indian scene.

Nabi Tanha said, "Thank you, Breshna jan," and pretended for a second to use it on his lips. Breshna Bahar made a sour smile at him.

"You idiot," she said sweetly.

In these rooms, once home to kings and queens, these actors and actresses moved with an air of noblesse as if this was where they, too, had always lived.

Soon it was almost time for the doors to be opened and let the audience come into the Queen's Palace. Corinne gathered the company together for their nightly pre-performance circle. By now, the actors had adopted the ritual as their own: closed eyes, deep breath, open eyes, and a resounding "*Merde!*" For most, this was the only French word they knew. They shouted it, and it echoed through the domed chambers of the *hamam*.

The boys quickly scampered across the terrace to the holding room that had been created for them in the other wing by draping large sheets of burlap in a few key places.

The doors to the Queen's Palace swung open, and the great and the good of Kabul began to enter.

20

The Light Garden of the Angel King

Kabul. September 4, 2005.

From our vantage point in the *hamam*, we could see the incoming audience as they emerged from the covered passage and stepped into the Queen's Palace garden for the first time. Nearly every one of them paused in amazement at what they saw. The garden was unlike any other public space they had previously encountered in Kabul.

Among those coming in were the ambassadors of France and Canada. The British ambassador had been called away, but his top aides were there. A few members of the American embassy staff came as well, but most of their colleagues had, per usual, been restricted to their compound.

The British Council had arranged the security for the evening, but had done so very carefully and subtly. No guns or uniforms were in sight. No one was searched on the way in, as was common when going into most office buildings even in those relatively peaceful days. But a team was firmly in place to ward off any problems. There were none.

Several members of the family of the former king, Zahir Shah, came. They were as thrilled as everyone else by the work of the Aga Khan Trust for Culture in bringing the old palace's eclectic combination of Afghan and classical architecture back to life. Though it had once been owned by their family, many of them had never been there before. They walked all around the terrace and the garden, enjoying the view of the mountains through the arched openings in the western wall.

A couple of Cabinet ministers and many junior ministers of the Afghan government arrived, some with their families. Leading Afghan businessmen showed up in large numbers, including Rahim Walizada who graciously made light of the dust that his carpets were gathering.

"*Mushkel nast,*" he said. "No problem. A little dust never hurt an Afghan carpet."

Staff from several international aid projects came, many with their Afghan colleagues. One of them was Sue Nicholson who managed an educational programme with her husband, Simon, for the British charity Children in Crisis. She had brought a group of Afghan teachers with her. The teachers hailed from Kandahar, Farah, Laghman and Kunduz provinces – all very conservative areas. The Nicholsons had been holding training sessions for them in Kabul that week. None of the teachers had ever attended a play before, and were taking in the scene around them with undisguised delight.

Many of the younger international aid workers sat with young Afghans on the *toshaks* laid out in front of the chairs.

As the time for the performance approached, a wave of Afghan men who worked in the Bagh-e-Babur came in and took seats along the edge of the terrace to the right of the entry. Others sat on the steps of the grand staircases. Some had brought their children. More came. They filled the side terraces. Some came down and sat in the chairs. And still more came as the performance progressed.

The performance's starting time came and went. The start had to be delayed as the flood of people coming in continued. Unlike the Foundation, there was room here for everybody. More chairs were located from somewhere, and set up. Some people chose to stand, with the standees in some places being three-deep behind the chairs.

Finally, with the stucco of the palace turning a golden red in the setting sun, Corinne and Qais walked to the centre of the stage to welcome everyone. And then the play began.

∾

With a great sense of authority, the King of Kabul came forth from the boys' holding room, strode across the terrace and made his way down the wide stone stairs. He mounted his carpet-covered *takht* and slowly surveyed the crowd, just as a real king might. The audience responded with utter silence, as if they were truly in a royal presence. Shah Mohammed had been a king for four nights, now. He had begun to enjoy being the most important man in the story, even more important than his teacher and friend Nabi Tanha, at least for these few hours during the play. He drew himself up, and spoke the first line announcing the vow that he and his friends had made.

Corinne had worked with the actors that afternoon on projecting their voices. She had been concerned that coming from the relatively compact quarters of the Foundation's garden, they would have trouble being heard across the wide expanses of these palace gardens. Shah Mohammed spoke crisply and clearly. From the back of the standees, we could hear everything he said.

As he finished, the boys ceremoniously made their way down the stairs in single file, and took their places on the *kilims*. Their entrance entranced the audience. Stylised processions, even a small one like this one, are uncommon in Afghan culture.

The first joke was coming soon. Over the course of the four previous performances, we had discerned that the response to that joke predicted the reaction of the audience for the rest of the play. If they laughed shyly, they would grin at the other jokes, but repress any real laughter. If they chuckled audibly, then they would laugh a little louder every time until they could fully unleash their laughter during the Bollywood scene.

The joke came. Arif said his line, and gave his look of astonishment. We did not have to wait long for a response. The Queen's Palace rocked.

All the workmen up on the terraces and the steps and standing around the perimeter exploded in laughter. That ignited the Afghans in the seats who may have felt more restrained, but now clapped and laughed and looked at each other in delight, and laughed some more. The eyes of the actors sparkled. They had never had a response like this. Then the audience instantly grew quiet, as they hung on every word, until they erupted even more loudly with the next joke, even though it was not as funny as the first one. We looked at each other in amazement.

The girls entered. But we really could not call them girls anymore, not with the profound dignity with which they were all carrying themselves. As they descended the other flight of stairs, they and their costumes never looked more exquisite. The fabric appeared incandescent in the last full rays of the day's sunlight. Perhaps a grand arrival by the ladies on camels would have been more theatrical, but it could not have been more spectacular. As always, a sense that something remarkable was happening fell over the crowd as the women joined the men on stage.

In an unfortunate coincidence owing to our delayed start, the *azan* sounded for the prayers at sunset just as the women reached the playing area. For a few moments, "the audience fell guiltily silent," one British journalist wrote later. But the actors did not miss a beat, even as several men wearing elaborate turbans got up from their chairs and turned their backs on the actors. Were they protesting the presence of the women? Had no one explained what they were going to be seeing?

The men made their way to an open area near the western wall, spread their neck scarves on the ground and commenced their prayers. When they had finished, they shook the dust out of their scarves, went back to their seats and resumed watching the play, which had continued while they had prayed.

In a country where some men stop to pray as soon as they hear the *azan* even if they are standing by the side of the road with traffic whizzing past them, it was not out of the ordinary for these men to break away from the performance for a few minutes to fulfill their religious obligations. Nor was it unusual that many other men chose not to pray at that time, but would wait until later, after the performance had ended.

∾

All the actors were in top form. None had so completely inhabited their roles before as they were doing in this performance. Parwin and Kabir as the hapless go-betweens for the noblemen and noblewomen, were flawless. They drew big laughs for comic business that had never worked as well before.

Sabah Sahar and Breshna Bahar, who by day were enforcers of laws in an often lawless land, had that night become royal ladies in the truest sense. Their commanding presence resonated with the protocols of the ancient court of Herat, long the seat of learning and the arts in Afghanistan. Marina giggled only on cue, and was deeply moving when she was meant to be. Her work in films had taught her how to draw focus by being still.

Leila's mock swooning over Faisal's Mansour adroitly pushed the comedy to the edge of the absurd, but never over it. Consciously or unconsciously, she had obviously been studying her father's perfect timing and deft touch in his political satire skits on television.

Faisal's gift for guileless hamming was her perfect foil. He made his character self-important without ever becoming that way himself. Perhaps because he had so many self-doubts.

Arif was especially electrifying. Instead of hiding on a tree, as he had at the Foundation, he somehow climbed inside one of the towering arches. He loomed above the other actors in the garden far below, reacting with amazement at their clumsy efforts to hide. It was hard for the audience to take their eyes off him. Throughout the rest of the evening, he glowed with an energy that made him more spellbinding than he ever had been before.

As the actors performed, first one, then another and another youngster began to appear on the perimeter wall behind the terrace and its arches. How had they gotten up there? The wall was easily twenty feet high above the street. Had someone brought a ladder? That wall had been built by kings to keep armies out. Yet these kids, like human kites, had managed to fly themselves on top of it.

They were probably too far away to hear the actors well, but the roar of the crowd kept them transfixed. Behind them, as had happened at the Foundation, the mud houses on the hills began to turn on their lights. This neighbourhood had electricity, though at a low voltage. The soft light of underpowered, unshaded bulbs glowed through a thousand windows.

Meanwhile the floodlights that we had placed around the garden were beginning to isolate the playing area from its magnificent surroundings as it replaced the fading daylight. That had the effect of drawing the audience ever more deeply into the story. The colours in the four *kilims* and the carpets on the *takht* took on an extra richness against the dust and the stone battlements.

With the growing darkness, the number of workmen seated on the grand staircases swelled. First there were only a few of them, then one or two on every step. Before long, the steps were filled as if they had been designed as a grandstand.

By the time the Bollywood scene started, it was fully dark and the actors looked like rock stars in megawatt stage lighting. The audience went wild the moment Nabi Tanha appeared. This night he had fastened his *dhoti* with a safety pin to keep it from slipping off, as it nearly had two nights before leaving him grabbing its cotton lengths to cover his plaid boxer shorts.

Nabi Tanha began to sing, and the audience started making so much noise that few could really hear him at all. Applause for Nabi Tanha is like a drug. The more he hears, the more exuberant his performance. The song went on for several extra verses. When Faisal followed him, they cheered even more. And so it went.

Nobody could hear how bad a singer Arif was that night. As soon as he started his song, many in the audience started singing it with him. In the impromptu gallery along the side terraces, workmen in the audience were dancing with their arms flung out and their hands in the air.

By now the standees were all pushing forward. They wanted to hear and see everything better, to be part of things. The neat aisles we had laid out where the men could chase the women were completely clogged. We knew that the chase scene was coming, and we tried to move enough people out of the way so that the performers could run through the crowd and get back to the playing area. Nobody wanted to move.

Nabi Tanha and Breshna were the first to run. Perhaps because they were respected by most of the audience as Bulbul and Gul Chaira, the standees instinctively opened a space for them. As they raced towards the back of the audience, we made big gestures pointing to their left, so they would know where to go. They were moving too fast to stop and ask directions. We ran along side them, guiding them through the crowd and back towards the stage.

The audience was as energised by the chases as they had been for the Bollywood scene. The workmen up on the terraces were shouting at the running couples as if they were placing bets on some kind of race.

With the dramatic arrival of Mustafa Haidari as the Messenger from Herat, the play entered its quieter final minutes. The audience acted relieved to have a little rest. They listened carefully as the men expressed their affection and intentions for the women, and as the women gently deflected them, at least for one year. And then the final line: "So now, you that way: we this way."

The girls walked from the playing area and up the grand stairs to an ear-shattering roar of approval from the crowd of a kind that they may never hear again. Hundreds and hundreds of clapping hands and cheering voices. The boys were blocked from leaving, as the stairs down which they had first entered were now entirely filled by spectators. So they stood there smiling until the women returned to take a bow. And bow. And bow. And bow. The audience did not want to let them stop.

As they had done at the Foundation, the actors sat on the *takht* platform and sang a few songs. More clapping. More cheering. More singing, until finally they were able to make their way back up to the *hamam* and their dressing room. Under those elaborately plastered domes, they shrieked their delight and hugged one another. None of them had ever experienced anything like this before.

They started singing. Indian songs. Afghan songs. Beatles songs. Any kind of song they knew as they hung their costumes back on the racks.

At the lower end of the garden below them, the tall doors in the Queen's Palace gatehouse swung open to save the audience from having to climb the grand stairs to the terrace to get out through the covered passage. But many seemed to want to do that anyway, to extend for a few more minutes the sense of enchantment that had been created there that night. Slowly the audience filed out into the magnificent gardens that Babur had laid out so carefully only a few decades before Shakespeare had written *Love's Labour's Lost*.

One of the Afghan teachers who had come with Sue Nicholson, Shaqib from Kandahar, was greatly disappointed that it was the show's last performance, because he wanted to come back again the next night. Sayed from Laghman said, with his eyes alight, that he had never in his fifty years seen anything like it.

Beatrice Litt, a native of Sicily working in the U.S. embassy, was jubilant. "As I entered into the walled garden of the Queen's Palace, I felt like I was back home in the ancient Greek theatre in Siracusa in my beautiful Sicilia, though perhaps we had a little bit less dust there!" she joked.

One man gushed to Jolyon Leslie that he had watched a smiling French Ambassador in the front row "leaning out of his chair to hear every word though he does not know Dari, the children thronging the stairways, the masons hanging off the balcony, with the sun setting through the dust of Kart-e-Seh, and then Sohrab hiding above in a great ruined arch, with ragged burlap drapes hanging down. You could not have designed a more dramatic set for a million dollars."

The good words followed Corinne, the actors and everyone else involved with the production to a rooftop terrace at the corner of the Queen's Palace that we had not seen before. Malcolm Jardine had chosen it as the site for the reception being given by the British Council. It overlooked the rest of Babur's magnificent garden, so aptly described by his great-grandson, Shah Jahan, as "the light garden of the Angel King."

All of Malcolm's distinguished Afghan and foreign guests were gathering there, enjoying the fine Afghan food laid out for them, along with many kinds of freshly squeezed fruit juices. Hundreds of candles flickered all around. It was an occasion as ethereal as everything else that had happened that evening, and a triumph for the British Council.

The unpretentious son of a Scottish farmer, Malcolm Jardine was in his element, bringing together people from different cultures, from all strata of their respective societies, making introductions and connections that would long be fueled by the good feelings of that evening. Not only had he enthusiastically embraced the commitment of his predecessor, Richard Weyers, to fund the production, he had even found additional funds when we discovered that we needed more.

The words of praise kept coming. The actors were laughing. Corinne was happier than we had ever seen her. Despite all the obstacles, she had somehow managed to will this unlikely creature called *Love's Labour's Lost* into existence, and then drive it to success. No one knew the challenges she had overcome better than we did. No one was in greater awe of what she had done than we were.

21

Applause

Kabul. September 8, 2005.

The dust settled in the Bagh-e-Babur, but the glow of our evening there hung in the air for days after.

Corinne prepared to leave for Paris, amid hugs and tears from her cast. Marina Gulbahari was inconsolable. She sobbed, saying over and over, "You are my director," while hanging on to Corinne, as if trying to keep her from going to the airport. In Afghan culture, to be addressed by a title such as "Doctor" or "Engineer" or "Teacher" is regarded as a high honour. To be called "Director" is no different.

Even Nabi Tanha, who had never hesitated to challenge Corinne on just about anything, was now describing her as a "great director, a wonderful woman. She is my good friend."

It was good to be free of the pressures of having to get all the actors together every day, to comfort those who were sick, arrange rides for those coming late, listen to their complaints and see that Corinne had everything she needed. But our peace was interrupted, in a most unexpected way.

For the next several weeks, we were approached by many university-aged guys who had seen the play. Like most Afghans, they were hungry for knowledge. They wanted to know everything we could tell them about *Love's Labour's Lost*. They had no idea who Shakespeare was.

By then, we had finally received copies from Iran of Dr. Alaeddin

Pazargadi's two-volume Farsi translations of the complete works of Shakespeare. A couple of the plays had also been published in individual editions. We let some of the young guys borrow those. They passed them all around, from one to the next; everybody wanted to read all of them.

Several of them also asked to read our Dari script for *Love's Labour's Lost*. We gave them an extra copy that we had. One young man photocopied it. Then he photocopied his photocopy to give to a friend who photocopied that one. Another guy photocopied that one, and gave it to someone else. Over the next few weeks, so many copies of copies had been made that it was almost impossible to read them.

We asked one of the young guys who had already read all the individual editions and still wanted to read more, why he liked Shakespeare so much. He told us, "He makes you laugh in one eye, and cry in the other."

∽

In the weeks before the opening night, we had been contacting the foreign journalists in Kabul to tell them what we were doing. Meanwhile, Timor Hakimyar and Robert Kluijver were dong the same with many leading Afghan journalists. Press releases and invitations were sent to all of them. Several reporters did stories, some even before the show opened.

In a lengthy feature in *The Christian Science Monitor*, reporter Scott Baldauf captured why we believed that Shakespeare would be entertaining to Afghan audiences:

> There is much about modern-day Afghanistan, emerging from twenty-three years of war, that William Shakespeare would have found familiar: autocratic leaders playing great games with the lives of men, doomed lovers defying ethnic or tribal taboos, nobles and servants trading bawdy jokes, and devious warlords and ambitious mistresses hatching foul plots.

Baldauf described Faisal as "the handsome actor who plays the nobleman, Dumain." When we spotted that, we quickly showed it to

Faisal, who beamed. He asked over and over again, "Show me where it says that?" We highlighted it in yellow for him, even though he could not read the English words. He walked around holding it as if he had been given the one thing he had always wanted most.

Andrew North of the BBC did some interviews with Corinne and members of the cast a few weeks before the first performance. With Australian videographer Sophie Barry, he captured the sense of impending excitement in the days leading up to the opening. He particularly wanted to interview Marina, since she was well-known to audiences around the world from the film *Osama*.

The interview took longer than it might have owing to Marina's inevitable fits of giggles that had to be allowed to pass. Despite all her film work, she was too shy to look into the camera to answer personal questions. Eventually, she relaxed and spoke of what she had learned from the production.

The report aired on BBC Worldwide Television on the morning of the performance at the Bagh-e-Babur. It was widely seen by the international community in Kabul and probably motivated many of them to come.

Kim Barker, then *The Chicago Tribune's* correspondent for South Asia, attended the first performance at the Foundation. She captured all that hung in the balance:

> Before the play opened Wednesday, everyone involved was worried. Would Afghans come? Would women come? Would the actors and actresses be safe? Would cast members remember their lines? Would a fight break out onstage, as it had in rehearsal? Would people in the audience laugh? More importantly, would they get it?

Rachel Morarjee, reporting for Agence France Presse (AFP), attended the opening night performance. The story that she filed was carried in papers all around the world the next day.

> Afghanistan's first public performance of a Shakespeare play in a quarter-century raised delighted laughter from a packed house this week, with most of the audience having never seen live theatre before, much less men and women acting together.

"It's the first time I've ever seen anything like this in my life and I really loved it. Especially when the boys did Indian dances," said Rafi Aria, a 24-year-old singer who performs on Afghan television and sings at weddings.

She went on to add that "this would have been unheard of under the Taliban regime." The new Afghanistan was taking shape in the garden of the Foundation for Culture and Civil Society. She quoted Leila as saying, "I was very nervous before we began the performance, but when people in the audience started laughing and clapping, I knew they were happy."

The AFP story attracted the attention of editors around the world. Those with correspondents in Kabul asked them to write something about the production. Many of the foreign media corps showed up at the final performance at the Bagh-e-Babur.

The correspondent for *The Daily Telegraph* in London, Tom Coghlan, quoted Faisal as saying the Taliban would "never allow us to put on a play, to tell a story about love. Now we have a democracy, and we can show these things to our people. I am so proud."

That was a message that resonated through newsrooms all over the world. Suddenly, Shakespeare in Kabul was a hot news story. Very political.

The Associated Press distributed a report filed by Daniel Cooney that was translated into several languages and picked up by newspapers on every continent but Antarctica on September 8th. It was carried by *The New York Times*, *USA Today*, *The Boston Globe* and countless others. That same day, the BBC World Service aired a radio story about the production which was heard even in Antarctica. Seven continents in one day, we thought. Not bad. Our fifteen minutes of fame.

Cooney's story captured the visceral excitement felt by many in the audience who saw the production as a celebration of the end of the Taliban era:

The actresses do not hide behind veils or all-encompassing *burqas*, like most women on the streets outside. The young characters also openly flirt – taboo in a country where men and women are not supposed to speak to each other unless they are related.

There are passionate declarations of love and hearts' desires, unusual for most young Afghan couples, whose marriages are arranged by parents who rarely consider matters of affection.

It's hardly a tale the Taliban would have approved, but judging by the cheers and whoops, many in the audience did.

Several of the media reports mentioned the Indian scene, and the audience's hearty response to it. One noted that "by the time the actors dressed up as Indians and mimicked Bollywood song-and-dance routines, the audience was laughing hysterically. People spontaneously started to clap, although it was only the middle of the show."

A few days later, even the staid British weekly magazine *The Economist* waxed poetic about the production, headlining it: "a magic performance in a dusty Afghan garden." Reporter James Astill summed up the achievement and the challenge of the production.

As in Shakespeare's comedies as in life, joy is tinged with sorrow. And no where more than in Afghanistan, where international efforts to heal the broken country are dogged by grief, after a quarter-century of war, and fear of what maybe to come when the peacekeepers depart. The wonderful production of *Love's Labour's Lost* that has just been running in Kabul – Afghanistan's first professional theatre since the fighting began – reflected this hard truth.

Astill ended his unexpected turn as a drama critic with a prescience born of his regular assignment as *The Economist's* Defence and Terrorism Correspondent.

In Afghanistan as in Shakespeare's comedies, the future is less rosily settled than it may seem. As it is said in *Love's Labour's Lost*: "Worthies, away! The scene begins to cloud."

22

Encores

Kabul, September 2005–April 2006.

Even before that final glorious evening at the Bagh-e-Babur, there was already talk about additional performances. Several government ministers had seen the production. Some had come back for a second look with their families. A couple of them said that they wanted to bring *Love's Labour's Lost* to their Ministries so their workers could enjoy it, especially the women who were not as free to attend public performances.

The Minister of Women's Affairs was especially eager, saying, "I want my people to see what Afghans can do." Those from the U.S. Embassy who had managed to get to see the show wanted us to do a performance on the embassy's lawn for all their colleagues who had missed it. Other performances were mentioned for two orphanages in Kabul, one for girls and one for boys that together were home to more than 1,400 children.

Someone suggested that we do a performance at the war-damaged Kabul Theatre, built by the Germans. Its managers encouraged us to come, stating that a performance there would have been a great vote of confidence in the future of the performing arts in Kabul. We could also help them raise the funds and public awareness they needed to put the theatre back together.

A date was even proposed for a return engagement to the Bagh-e-Babur.

In the end, however, no additional performances took place that year. Afghanistan's first parliamentary elections were scheduled to be held about two weeks after the show closed. There were widespread concerns – unfounded, as it turned out – that those opposed to democratic government in Afghanistan might engage in terror tactics in the run-up to the voting. Public performances, especially of a western-inspired show, were seen as possible targets.

Also, the holy month of Ramazan would be starting shortly after the elections. Practically speaking, no performances could be given until Ramazan had ended. By then, cool weather and shorter days would have made outdoor performances problematic.

Corinne, back in Paris, was reluctant for the actors to perform without her being with them. The charm and excitement of the evening at the Bagh-e-Babur may have distracted the audience from a few small flaws in the performance, but they had not escaped Corinne's sharp eye. She was concerned that the actors, without her directorial guidance, might perform the play badly, and cool the excitement it was generating. Also, as a theatre professional, she knew how fragile a production can be when it gets moved to a new venue.

Others argued that performances organised by the actors themselves would show that they had taken ownership of the project. Since they would be playing to uncritical audiences at the ministries and orphanages, the high standards Corinne sought to maintain were perhaps not required.

It was a moot argument. We needed about $6,000 for a half-dozen performances, but the donors we approached had exhausted their available funding, and the Ministries had none for cultural events like this. But an idea had been planted.

The wave of cheering media reports that kept arriving during the next few weeks fertilised it. A prominent citrus grower in Florida named Frank Bouis, who had read James Astill's report in *The Economist*, sent a check for $1,000 to support future performances of the production. Almost immediately, ideas about a national tour the following year were floated.

A producer for the Canadian Broadcasting Corporation (CBC) had heard about the production and wanted to make a one-hour documentary on it. She proposed bringing a crew to Kabul in the summer of 2006. She contacted Malcolm Jardine at the British Council, who passed her request on to us.

Separately, the French periodical *Marie Claire* had been in touch with Corinne wanting to do an in-depth article if she were to be mounting the production again. And one of the Afghan television networks, Afghan National Television, expressed interest in taping the entire production for broadcast. That level of media interest would bring *Love's Labour's Lost* to a vast audience. We started soliciting funding.

~

A new proposal for the production to be remounted in 2006 was written. It stated confidently that performances would take place in Kabul "in Afghan government ministries, at foreign embassies and in public parks. Performances in the provinces are expected to take place in Pul-i-Khumri, Tashqurgan, Kunduz, Mazar-e-Sharif, Sherbighan, and Herat."

The British Council's Malcolm Jardine, truly a greater hero of *Love's Labour's Lost* than any of the nobles depicted by Shakespeare, stepped forward immediately and offered to provide almost half of the $35,000 we had budgeted for the Afghanistan tour. The British Council operated programmes in several Afghan cities, and was keen to have the production visit them.

He stressed though, that the British Council was funding a large array of new programmes in Afghanistan that year. It could not support *Love's Labour's Lost* to the extent that it had the previous year. Understood. We expectantly approached several other donors.

The Goethe Institut, which had provided some urgently needed funding the year before to cover a budget shortfall, had already committed all its available funds. We made a strong pitch to the Canadian Embassy, stressing the planned visit by the CBC. They said they had no funds for cultural events.

Those staff from the U.S. Embassy in Kabul who had attended the performance in the Bagh-e-Babur and had raved about it to their colleagues, were finishing their one-year rotation in Kabul, and were heading home. Their replacements had neither seen the production nor experienced the buzz it had sent through Kabul.

Three of the new staff at the U.S. Embassy came to the Foundation to meet the actors, and see a few scenes from the play performed for them. They offered heartfelt applause and words of encouragement, but no funds. The problem, they said, was that Shakespeare was not an American writer, and they are mandated by Congress to use their funds to promote American culture. At first we thought they might be joking. But they were not. They would have liked to have helped if it had been up to them, they said, but their hands were tied.

In the end, Malcolm Jardine found a couple of thousand more dollars, and *Love's Labour's Lost* went back into full production. Without his help, everything would have ended right there. Still, the tour had to be cut back. It was limited to Herat and Mazar-e-Sharif, where the British Council's local programmes could provide support. Kunduz and some of the other places we had considered were maybe a bit too socially conservative, anyway.

Actors want to perform. Even though several shows in Kabul were being planned, no one was happy with the shortened tour. Still, the level of excitement remained high.

∾

Corinne came back in early May, and reunited the cast for a picnic in the garden that surrounds the old fort where she was again staying. Several Balouch carpets had been laid in the grass in the shade of an old tree. Platters of food were brought out. Nabi Tanha played the harmonium and declaimed *ghazals*, the great lyric poems of the Indo-Persian world. Shah Mohammed accompanied him on a *tabla*. Everyone sang. It was a good beginning.

Over the next few days, however, Corinne discovered that two of the girls were not going to be available after all.

Marina Gulbahari was committed to making a film near Bamyan during that summer. Corinne tried hard to accommodate her schedule. Many long conversations were held with Marina and her film director, Siddiq Barmak, but no agreement could be reached.

Sabah Sahar had to go to Germany during the summer, and would not be in Afghanistan at the time of the performances. She also said that she had suffered some public criticism as a result of having been in the show the year before, and that her husband was reluctant to allow her to do it again.

While that might have been unexpected from a woman who regularly appeared in videos, things in Afghanistan work by their own logic; family opinions carry great weight. Corinne held several sessions with her, and with her husband, trying to find a way to work around these problems, but to no avail.

Corinne now faced the unexpected need to find two new actresses with only about two weeks before the first scheduled performance.

༄

Rehearsals started with the actors who were there. The actors all seemed to have forgotten their lines, but not their grudges.

One day early on, the actors decided to tease Corinne. At the beginning of the rehearsal, they ran through a scene and made a total mess of it. Corinne launched into a long explanation of what the scene was all about, what their characters were supposed to be doing. She asked the actors many questions to try to understand why they had forgotten their lines, or their moves, or their cues.

When what she had said was translated, the actors burst out laughing. They told Corinne to sit and watch. Then they ran through the whole scene perfectly. An Afghan joke.

༄

Breshna Bahar's teen-age daughter, Wazhma, had seen every performance and many rehearsals the year before. She knew nearly everybody's lines. Though she was a bit shy, in the way all Afghan girls are taught to be, Corinne sensed that Wazhma's years of exposure to her mother's performing career had given her skills that were not immediately apparent.

One day, she asked Wazhma if she would take over the role of Senober that had been played by Marina Gulbahari. Wazhma was stunned, and could barely reply. Her mother was the actress in the family, not her. She had to think about it, she said. In the meantime Corinne asked her to help by reading Marina's lines during the rehearsals. It was a subtle ploy, and it worked. Within a few days, Wazhma was a full member of the cast.

The search for an actress to assume Sabah Sahar's role as the Princess of Herat was more complicated. Corinne met with several actresses. The days passed, the pressure mounted, but no one she saw seemed to be right for the role. Briefly she considered performing it herself, if no one could be found.

Finally, she encountered Amina Jaffari, who had appeared in many Afghan television programmes and films, and looked the part of a noblewoman. More importantly, she showed good instincts as a performer when Corinne auditioned her.

Special sessions were arranged for her for three mornings at the old fort so she could become familiar with the play and have some help learning her lines. In the end she had only about a week of rehearsals with the rest of the actors. But she was a quick study, even of Shakespeare's poetry, and we sensed that she would do well.

∾

The CBC crew arrived. Their cameraman shot many hours of footage during rehearsals. They conducted interviews with cast members and Corinne during breaks. By their presence, they generated a sense of anticipation. Everyone felt part of something very important. But the distraction of the camera and the interviews slowed down the integration of the two new actresses into the production.

Nabi Tanha did not immediately accept having Amina in the cast, for reasons that were never entirely clear. He did another walkout, as he had the year before. Corinne shrugged off his departure, and said he would come back. She went on rehearsing without him. Two days later, he returned. There was no time to waste talking about whatever had annoyed him. He rejoined the rehearsals, as if he had been there all along.

Meanwhile Amina and Shah Mohammed suffered sprained ankles, and could barely limp, with only a few days left to get the show back on its feet. Then we lost a full day quite unexpectedly owing to a tragic incident that led to anti-foreigner riots on May 28, and a tense atmosphere for many days after.

An American military vehicle had lost its brakes while coming down a steep hill on the outskirts of Kabul. It plowed into a crowd of shoppers near a large open-air bazaar at Khair Khana, killing several Afghans. When an angry crowd surrounded the truck, some of the soldiers inside panicked and opened fire. As word spread across the city, mobs materialised and randomly attacked buildings that evoked the presence of foreigners, from Chinese brothels and CARE International's compound to a pizza shop, though it was owned by Afghans.

At the time of the incident, we were in the bazaar where tents are made and sold. We had not been able to locate Hashmat Ghani Ahmadzai, from whom we had again hoped to borrow his attractive six-sided tent. He had stood for election to Parliament the previous September and had lost. He had left Kabul for a while.

While a tentmaker was stitching pieces together to our specifications with his foot-powered sewing machine, Malcolm Jardine called to tell us about the incident at Khair Khana. We decided to head home straight away.

In retrospect, the riots were the first tangible indication that things in Afghanistan had changed since our moment of unbridled optimism in the Bagh-e-Babur. At the time, though, we saw it as just an unfortunate event, and focused on getting our show up and running.

The riots also had one unexpected effect on the show.

When we had had to leave the tent makers bazaar sooner than expected, the man working on our tent did what he could as fast as he could. But he was unable to give the material we had purchased from him the fine, six-sided elegance of the tent we had borrowed the previous year.

Corinne did not pay attention to the tent until it was set up for the first time at the dress rehearsal. Then, when she saw its bright Turkmen colors and broad designs in place of whatever she was expecting, she vociferously and emphatically declared it "objectively ugly." Everybody else seemed to like it, but she was the director.

She made her peace with the tent by draping our much-used, and now much-loved Hazaragi *kilim* over it. To many of us, it looked like the *kilim* was being aired out on a strangely-shaped frame. By now, in fact, it needed that, along with a good washing.

෴

The first performance, held once again in the garden of the Foundation, was a bit shaky, as Amina and Wazhma felt their way. Though Wazhma was very good, she had never been on the stage before. She spoke very softly, timidly. Later, she noted feeling extremely self-conscious when the girls had to exchange their headscarves and for a moment she was standing in front of the men in the audience with her head uncovered; she had never done that before.

Amina had a bearing that suited her perfectly as the Princess of Herat. But having had so little rehearsal time, she not surprisingly felt adrift a few times, especially in the early moments. The other members of the cast covered for her, and guided her as needed. By the time she spoke the memorable closing line, she had taken total control of her part.

A couple of the other actors stumbled a time or two, as well. Probably no one in the audience was aware of any problem, but the missed cues and flubbed lines put the actors on notice. They knew that they had a huge reputation to live up to. In subsequent performances, they did. Indeed, the ability of cast members to cover the mistakes of others showed how deeply the sense of being part of a company had taken hold.

At a performance that was held in the garden of the old fort where Corinne was again staying, the actors performed around a large fountain. We worked out a comic moment for Shah Mohammed, Nabi Tanha and Faisal. We suggested that Shah Mohammed as the King of Kabul should show his displeasure that the other two had broken their vow by dunking their heads into the fountain.

Corinne thought it was vulgar, and was against doing it. The actors liked the idea, though, and did it anyway. The audiences roared. We looked at Corinne from the corner of our eyes as the heads were going into the fountain. She was laughing hard along with everyone else, including Prince Mirwais, the youngest son of the former King, Zahir Shah.

෴

That was the second time the Prince had attended the play. He had seen it a few nights earlier at the Foundation, but had to leave there immediately afterwards for a very important meeting at the palace, the Arg, as the complex where the King's palace is called. He had called his driver more than an hour before to arrange a pick-up. But it was still rush hour, given the play's early starting and ending times, and the streets were in total gridlock. His driver was stuck somewhere. He pleaded with us to find him a car that would get him to the Arg very quickly. The King was waiting.

Someone beckoned to Daoud, and introduced him to the Prince. He explained the situation to Daoud, and instructed him, "Daoud, be Daoud."

Prince Mirwais asked what that meant, and was told, "As you will soon see, sir, Daoud is the best driver in Kabul, and he is at his very best in rush hour."

The Prince looked hopeful, but unconvinced, and said politely to Daoud, "Can we get to the Arg in ten minutes." It was no great distance, and without traffic could easily be reached by then. Daoud looked at Prince Mirwais, and said with his ever-present luminous smile, "Of course. Let's go, and not waste time." Prince Mirwais smiled, too, and appeared to relax a bit. Daoud has that effect on everyone. They left.

Seven minutes later, a phone call came from Prince Mirwais, "You really do have the best driver in Kabul. I am home already. Can Daoud be my driver when you no longer need him?" he asked.

Prince Mirwais said we should perform the play in garden of the Arg so his father could see it. Zahir Shah, then ninety-three years old, was no longer the King of Afghanistan, as the monarchy had been abolished by the Communist government of the 1980s. But he had been given the title of Father of the Nation, and was held in respect by Afghans.

Zahir Shah said he would be happy to welcome the actors to the Arg. Unfortunately, his health declined soon after, and it became impossible for him to do so. But the royal endorsement of the production added an element of glamour.

∽

In all, we did five performances in Kabul, with three at the Foundation, one at the old fort, and one at the Bagh-e-Babur, but not in the Queen's Palace as the year before. Instead, we used the caravanserai that had been under construction near the main gate of the gardens on our first visit. The arched galleries the Aga Khan Trust for Culture had constructed to enclose a courtyard was ideal for our play. It was grand and intimate at the same time.

That was our last performance in Kabul. By then, all the actors were sure in their roles, and the performance had developed a very tight pacing

~

A few days later, the actors were all set to fly to Herat to start the tour. The CBC crew was eager to film the performance there. It had been scheduled to be staged in the ancient Citadel that had been sacked by Tamburlaine, the same tyrant depicted by Shakespeare's contemporary, Christopher Marlowe. In an irony with echoes of present-day Afghanistan, Marlowe was brought up on charges of blasphemy a few years later, and then was mysteriously murdered.

The day before we were set to depart, however, the Governor of Herat unexpectedly raised objections, and forbade the performances.

Herat is a remarkable city that is unlike any other in Afghanistan. At many times in history it has been part of the Persian empire. Its magnificent 13th century mosque, its gardens, its covered bazaars, its silk industry, its food and its accent all retain a distinctly Persian quality. That extends to politics. Herat province borders on Iran. That simple geopolitical fact causes its leaders to be very careful about anything that might stir up any problems.

The Governor, Sayed Hossein Anwari, had never heard of Shakespeare. What he knew was that we were proposing to have women appear on a stage in front of an audience that included men. Hence, the withdrawal of his earlier permission to let us perform there.

The CBC crew was thrown into a panic. They had to leave Afghanistan in just over a week. They had counted on the visuals of the Citadel to enhance their film. Long shots had been envisioned from the tops of its towers.

Jolyon Leslie and his team from the Aga Khan Trust for Culture were in the midst of a multi-year reconstruction of the Citadel, much as they had done at the Bagh-e-Babur in Kabul. They were prepared to provide much-needed logistical support supplying chairs and security to an audience that would be there by invitation.

A larger number of women would be in the audience than usual, since many of the women at Herat University would be attending as a group. We did not want to miss the chance to perform for them, or to see how they reacted.

We made phone calls to the Governor's office to plead our case. By amazing good fortune, we discovered that he had come to Kabul for the weekend. Leila mentioned that her father, Hanif Hamgam, was the Governor's good friend. Hanif jan offered to arrange a meeting for us with the Governor.

A group of us travelled to the Governor's house packed into a van driven by our good friend Ali Khan who holds the Governor in high regard. Both are Shi'a.

The Governor welcomed us into a large room where Ali Khan made a flowery speech expressing his respect for the Governor, whose hand he had kissed when we had first arrived. The Governor listened appreciatively. We drank many cups of tea, and made small talk about pleasant things. It would have been rude to just start discussing our business until we had been there for a while. Things were going well.

Then, a young American who was with us and was new to Afghanistan and did not understand Afghan customs, spoke out impatiently expressing her displeasure at the Governor's decision. The rest of us froze in embarrassment. The protocols had been broken. There was a collective holding of breaths.

The Governor laughed. We relaxed. He came to the point, and stated his concerns about allowing the show to happen. He listened as we explained everything that needed to be explained. But the Governor was still uncertain.

Then Ali Khan, who like Daoud has a gift for putting people at ease, started telling the Governor about the play, and about how people had laughed so much when they had watched it. The Governor listened intently, enjoying Ali Khan's descriptions of the jokes, the poetry and the Indian scene. He asked Ali Khan many questions about the production, which Ali Khan answered as if he himself had been the director. Suddenly, it was time for the Governor to go. He said he would let us know his decision in a few days. He gave Ali Khan a warm hug on the way out.

We left, not knowing whether we would be going to Herat. But we did know that we certainly would not be going there this week. The CBC crew freaked out. They needed to get footage of the tour for their documentary.

For Afghans, arranging something as complex as a performance in less than one week is not a big deal. That is how things are done in Afghanistan. Weddings to which three thousand or more guests are invited are generally announced only the day before they are held.

The Foundation had a representative in Mazar who agreed to set everything up for us. No problem, we were told. Everything has been organised. That settled it. We would head to Mazar so the CBC could get the footage they needed. We would go to Herat later, if the Governor allowed us.

The actors were pumped up when a couple of days later we piled into a pair of Kabul-Mazar highway taxi vans that the Foundation had hired for us, and headed north. Corinne was not able to come with us. The company of *Love's Labour's Lost* were "challenging the whole country" on their own.

23

Mazar-e-Sharif

Mazar-e-Sharif. May, 2006.

The eight-hour drive to Mazar crosses the Hindu Kush mountains through the Salang Tunnel, and then winds across the broad, arid valleys of northern Afghanistan until it finally unrolls on the flat steppe at the southern edge of Central Asia. This was the same road we had taken in the opposite direction from Mazar to Kabul the year before, when *Shakespeare in Kabul* was still an idea yet unformed. So much had happened since then.

Our actors are exuberant people. They love to sing, and laugh, and be mad at somebody. They all have to talk, often all at the same time. When we stopped for rest breaks, they all wanted to change vans, and did so several times. Most of the boys were wearing black T-shirts that somebody had given them.

One of the drivers was named Rahman. He could sing better and louder than the actors, which he did while speeding up and down the switchbacking mountain roads. Everyone wanted to be in his van. Nabi Tanha sat in the back seat hitting the *tabla* while Shah Mohammed in the front seat played the harmonium to accompany Rahman. The rest clapped from wherever they sat, led by Kabir.

Rahman had a rough voice, probably because he smoked nonstop, even while he was singing. Every time he lit a cigarette, he kept one between his lips, and gave others to the actors in the back seat. After every song, Nabi Tanha would shout out, "Oh, long life, Rahman, long life." Rahman would reply, "Nabi jan, let's play another song."

The CBC crew followed us in a van of their own. When we stopped in places like Salang, they came out with their cameras, and started filming. Sometimes they briefly interviewed one of the actors. Then we piled back in the vans, and began singing again.

As we reached the heights of Salang, Nabi Tanha took off his T-shirt, popped his head through an opening in the van's roof, though the air was freezing cold, and shouted, "This clean air is pure medicine. Inhale! Inhale to the bottom of your lungs, to the core of your heart, to the depths of your intestines!"

Everyone else was shivering, and shouted at him to close the roof, but Nabi Tanha was relishing his encounter with nature. He stayed aloft with his arms outspread as if he were on the prow of the Titanic waiting for Kate Winslet. Finally, he sat down and closed the roof, but only after we begged him to sing another song.

❧

We reached Mazar around 4:00pm. We went to the Hotel Mazar that had been booked for us. None of the rooms had a bathroom. We were expected to use a couple of communal bathrooms one floor below, shared by everyone else in the hotel. They were in bad shape, and smelled terribly.

There was no hot water, and sometimes no water at all. It was summer, and the wells were dry. The girls held up their hair, asking how could they shampoo in cold water.

As soon as we saw the dirty rooms, the old metal beds, the hard mattresses, stained pillows, soiled sheets, and layers of dust everywhere, we nervously asked ourselves, "If this is what is meant by 'everything has been organised,' where have they arranged for us to perform?"

A quick visit to the Foundation's Mazar office revealed that everyone there had gone home for the day, except for the director. After saying the usual pleasantries and drinking a glass of tea, we asked him if everything was ready. He looked at us, surprised, and asked, "Ready for what?"

"The chairs for the show," we said pleasantly, "and the tent, the security, the tea or water for the audience, the invitation cards, you know, everything? In fact, where is the show going to be held?"

"What is the rush for?" He looked at us as if we were crazy. "The show is next week."

"No, the show is not next week," we corrected him with the sort of smile that people use for jokes that are not funny. "It is the day after tomorrow."

"What?" The director showed us the printed invitation cards that were dated for the following week. No one had passed the word to him that, with the cancellation of the show in Herat, we were coming to Mazar a week earlier than planned.

"We are very sorry to have to tell you this," we told him as politely as we could, "but the actors are here. The show is the day after tomorrow." The director looked at us in wonderment, holding several now-useless invitation cards in his hand.

∽

The next day, everything had to be done. The brochures that had been printed with what was now the wrong date could not be used. We asked the director if he could get somebody with a loudspeaker in a truck to announce the show for the day after.

Done.

Then we went to a place where chairs are rented for weddings and made a deal to have a couple of hundred chairs delivered the following morning to Azadi Park in front of the Governor's Residence where the performance would be held.

Done.

We wanted to take a look at the park. Like most parks in Afghanistan, it has some tall pine trees, but no grass. Dust covers your feet when you walk in it. We could see that we would have to rent some cheap carpets to create a place for the actors to perform. Otherwise, they would choke when they tried to speak.

Done.

Then we went to the Mayor to tell him what we were doing, and to request that he provide security the next day. We had to wait for half

an hour for the Mayor to finish his meeting with a group of sports-
men who had just returned home from an international competition
with some medals.

The Mayor told us to talk with the Chief of Police. At the police
department, we drank tea for nearly an hour while waiting for the
chief to come. When he did, he was very polite, and asked endless
questions about the play: why were we doing it, was there anything
touchy in the show, why Shakespeare, why not an Afghan play, what
actors were in the play, what kind of security did we want, who
directed the play, why was the director not there, and were we making
excuses for her because there is something touchy in the play that
may reflect badly on her, and so on and so on.

The discussion went on for nearly an hour before the Chief of
Police gave his permission for the show to be performed, and started
making security arrangements.

∽

Meanwhile, the actors had decided to go to the blue-tiled shrine of
Hazrat Ali. Any Afghan coming to Mazar feels compelled to pray
there, and to walk through its gardens filled with roses and white
doves. But the peace that day was seriously disturbed.

Rahman saw what happened. He told us later that he had dropped
off the actors at the gate to the shrine's gardens, and had gone to park
the van in a shady spot. Shortly after, when he stepped out to buy
an orange from a street vendor, he noticed a large crowd gathering
inside the gardens. He kept straining his eyes in the glaring sunlight,
trying to see what was going on.

The last he had seen of Breshna Bahar and the girls, they had been
heading to find the Jogee women who sit on the sidewalks with their
babies tied to their backs, selling glass bracelets of many colours. The
Jogee women, with their grey eyes and well-tanned skin, are loud
when they talk, as if they are fighting. The pilgrims, men and women,
young and old, always haggle with them. Sometimes the haggling gets
interrupted when the police chase the Jogee women away; but five
minutes later they are back, after they have paid off the police to let
them remain for a few more hours.

"Suddenly," Rahman said, "I realised that it was Nabi Tanha and Breshna Bahar in the middle of the crowd. A mob of people were standing all around them, and shouting 'Bulbul! Bulbul!'" There were so many people that they could hardly move.

"They managed to get into the shrine, but by the time they had come out, even more people had gathered. They had to fight their way back to the van, and then I rushed them to the hotel to try to escape all their fans. But a lot of them ran after us.

"Soon, the word spread and I think everybody in Mazar came to stand outside the hotel hoping to get a glimpse of them. The security came to disperse the people. But they would not leave." That explained the crowd in the street we had had to push our way through to get into the hotel. Mostly it was young men in *shalwar kameez*, with a number of police standing nearby with sticks in their hands. They all seemed to be smiling, even the police.

Nabi Tanha's television series, *Bulbul*, had made stars out of him in the title role, and Breshna Bahar as his wife Gul Chaira. The series was one of the first Afghan programmes to hit the airwaves after the Taliban had left. Afghans could see lots of Indian and American programmes on Afghan television. But everyone loved *Bulbul*, because it was Afghan. It was about them.

"I was terrified," Breshna Bahar said later. "I really felt trapped by the crowd." Though she has stared down many vicious criminals in her police work, she said that nothing she had experienced as a policewoman had been as frightening. We had to go and buy *burqas* for her and the other girls so they could leave the hotel undetected. Nabi Tanha was forced to stay inside.

In Kabul, Nabi Tanha drives his motorcycle all over the city, usually with Shah Mohammed on the seat behind him. Nobody bothers him. Breshna Bahar drives her own car, which women do not do. Nobody bothers her. But in Mazar, the people do not see such celebrities very often, and so they became extremely excited.

Nabi Tanha sat in his hotel room, clearly shaken. He was nervous about what sort of crowd would come to the performance the next afternoon. Might there be a bomber among them? Nobody knew. Was there really any way to protect the actors on the stage? No one could say.

∾

The next day we went to Azadi Park early. The chairs arrived late, the carpets arrived late. No one came with the chairs to set them up in rows, or with the carpets to arrange them on the ground to make a stage. We had to set the whole place up ourselves. There was no tent where the actors could put on their costumes. They had to dress in the hotel, and come to the park ready to perform.

Two hours before the show, the park started filling up with people. Every chair was full, with at least two people on every seat. Hundreds of others were standing behind them, with still more in the trees. All their feet sent clouds of dust into the air. More than one thousand people were there. There were just too many of them. Many were workmen, people from the street who had heard the loudspeaker truck, but did not know what a play is. They just knew that Bulbul would be there.

The CBC crew were filming, amazed at what they were seeing.

For a short while before the actors arrived, the weather got windy and dust spun in small funnels through the park. We had some men sprinkle water on the ground around the performance area to damp down the dust. The security officers sent by the Chief of Police showed up, and kept asking questions. They were less interested in controlling the crowd than in seeing Bulbul and Gul Chaira, and having us take their pictures with them. We were feeling exhausted, because we had not had any lunch, and had been running like dogs since morning. But we felt that we had to be nice to the security men, and answer all their questions. They had guns.

As the crowd was filling the park, two women in *burqas* arrived and sat in chairs near the front, to one side. They were the only women there, apart from the actresses. Just before the show began, however, a man came and, without speaking to them, led them away. They made no attempt to argue, and left quietly, with the security men giving them a hand to climb a high step that led out of the park.

Finally, the show started. Nobody could hear what the actors were saying in the first scene in which only the men appear, because many in the audience kept shouting, "Bulbul, where is Gul Chaira?" And when Breshna Bahar finally appeared, they shouted even louder.

The actors performed all their scenes as they had rehearsed them, even though nobody in the crowd seemed to understand Shakespeare's poetry. For such an audience, something very simple would have worked better. Of course, the audience, which kept growing, loved the Indian scene the most. Some danced along with the actors.

As the performance proceeded, the actors began to relax. The crowd was huge, but it was friendly. It became apparent that if somebody were going to set off a bomb or interfere with the actors, they would have to deal with everybody else as well. Still, the boys had decided to take the precaution of wearing T-shirts with their *dhotis*, not certain whether local sensibilities might be offended by seeing bare-chested men.

At the end of the play, some of the audience rushed the stage to ask the actors for their autographs, especially Bulbul and Gul Chaira. They were so many that the security officers could not hold them back. Things quickly got out of control. With the help of a few Afghan soldiers, we pushed the actors one by one into the vans, and asked the drivers to go as fast as they could back to the hotel.

The crowd was so thick, though, that at first the vehicles could barely inch along. Rahman blasted his horn a couple of times, but that only made the crowd cheer. Then, slowly, they opened a path, and the vans began to move. Nabi Tanha sat in the front seat looking like a very important man, smiling and waving to the crowd, and shaking some hands through the open window.

CBC TV filmed the whole play, and the audience who had become as much a part of the show as the actors. They captured footage of kids hanging out of the trees, and of soldiers standing on army tanks nearby to get a good view. Later that evening, they invited us to the hotel where they were staying which was much better than ours, and hosted us for a grand dinner. By then Nabi Tanha and Amina had long ago become good friends, and along with everyone else, they enjoyed a joyful post-performance celebration of the largest audience we had ever had.

❧

The next morning we were scheduled to perform at a girl's school. The

British Council wanted to be sure that some women in Mazar had a chance to experience Shakespeare. When we arrived at the school, though, we discovered that the news had preceded us that Bulbul and Gul Chaira were on their way.

We had gone early to help set up an area for the performance in one corner of the schoolyard. It was not as dusty as Azadi Park, but we were using some of the same carpets we had used in the park the night before. The carpets sent up clouds of dust whenever anyone threw them on the ground.

When everything was ready, the actors arrived in their beautiful costumes. They all looked like they were going to a very fancy wedding party. The students, in their black school outfits and white head scarves, had been stealing looks whenever one of the crew had walked past their classrooms carrying things. While it was only us, the kids, though excited, did what the teachers told them to do.

Then they finally saw Bulbul and Gul Chaira, and their eyes grew wide. They made loud whispers to their friends. Within moments they were shrieking in delight. And, like a volcano, they erupted out of their classrooms and rushed into the schoolyard. Their teachers could do nothing to restrain them.

The students surrounded the actors for several minutes until the teachers started issuing orders, and got them to sit on the ground. But no one could stop the shrieking. The boys prepared to start the play. Amina and the other girls stood to one side waiting for their cue. The boys began the first scene, but no one could hear what they were saying. The kids were too excited to listen. The boys continued as best they could until the scene called for them to sing a song. Suddenly the students quieted.

By then the actors understood that doing a full performance was probably not going to be possible there that day. So instead, the girls joined the boys on stage. Together they sang all the songs in the play, along with a couple of others.

The students were thrilled, and cheered loudly when, after half an hour, the actors stood up to leave. Perhaps they had not experienced Shakespeare, but they had encountered the power of a live performance. Perhaps some seeds were planted that will one day take root in the new Afghanistan.

ᠬᠣ

Back in Kabul, the CBC crew said goodbye. They went back to Canada and made their documentary. They captured the hectic pace of our frantic rehearsals, and our wildly enthusiastic reception in Mazar. They also included some good interviews with the actors. Kabir said things to the CBC that he had never said to us, about how he believed our production of *Love's Labour's Lost* could really have a positive impact on Afghanistan. They structured the film around Corinne as she is a Canadian citizen, and gave her a much-deserved opportunity to talk about her experience in directing the production. Sadly, however, they never mentioned all the support we had received from the British Council, though we had asked them many times to do so.

24

Herat

Herat. May, 2006.

Within a week, we received word that the Governor of Herat would allow us to perform, but only as a private performance within the walls of the Citadel. Our hopes of doing the play in a large public park and at a girls school, as we had attempted to do in Mazar, were quashed.

The entire company took an afternoon plane to Herat, except for Corinne, who again stayed behind in Kabul. They mounted the stairs to the plane, waving like celebrities to Nabi Tanha on the tarmac who was videotaping everything. Faisal sported a necktie and, uncharacteristically, was clean shaven. He looked like businessman heading to a conference. For a few of the actors, it was their first time flying. They examined the safety cards with interest and kept their faces glued to the windows as the plane took off and lifted over the dusty, familiar streets of Kabul.

Leila's brother, Nazeef, travelled with us, as he had to Mazar. Leila was unmarried, and it would have been improper for her to travel without a male relative. Nazeef was one of us now. Mustafa Haidari had not been able to travel with the group, so Nazeef took over the small but pivotal role of the Messenger. He quickly demonstrated that he, indeed, comes from a family of actors. He knew just what to do.

The actors had been booked into the Mawfaq Hotel. The swimming pool had weeds growing through its cracks. The staff was run ragged bringing tea to the actors' rooms and responding to their endless requests. But they did not seem to mind since Bulbul and Gul Chaira were the most demanding, and they were famous. The rooms were marginally better than those in Mazar. By now, we knew what to expect when touring. At least we had water.

Nabi Tanha and Breshna Bahar stayed in the hotel, not wanting to risk repeating the mob scenes of Mazar. The others wandered in twos and threes through the neatly laid out streets of Herat, where the air was far cleaner than in Kabul. There were traffic lights, then unknown in Kabul, and, amazingly, the drivers actually obeyed them. Sidewalk bazaars sold everything from women's undergarments to switchblades. A long park ran in front of the hotel. It was filled with flowers and people sitting on the grass. Many of them sipped tea provided by push-cart vendors.

We walked into the old part of the city near the vast Jumaa Mosque that had been built in 1200. Its immense portal and towering minarets are covered with multicoloured tiles in deep shades of blue, yellow, pink and green, making a vast ceramic carpet. Its courtyard can hold more than a thousand worshippers. The marble paving stones in the courtyard was burning our bare feet until a young man suggested we walk only on the white marble. He was right. The white was much cooler. We were grateful, and invited him to the play the next day.

A young American writer named Jacob Baynham, who was visiting Afghanistan for the summer, had come to Herat with us. For several weeks, he had been living in Kabul in one of the guest rooms at the Foundation, and had been watching our rehearsals there every day.

While we were in the mosque, three men in their mid-thirties came over to talk to Jacob, though none of them could speak any English, except "hello" and "goodbye." They were dressed in *shalwar kameez*. One had a black turban with a long, black beard. Another wore a white prayer hat. And the third had thick black hair, combed backward. They were all the same height, but shorter than Jacob.

The man in the black turban asked Jacob, "Are you a *kharijee*, a foreigner?"

With the help of an interpreter, he told them, "Yes, I am. I'm an American."

"American!" they all exclaimed happily. The man with the white hat asked, "What are you doing here?"

"Visiting your beautiful country," Jacob said with a smile. They all nodded their heads in approval.

"Are you a Christian?" the man with the turban asked.

"I was raised Christian," Jacob replied.

The man with the thick black hair then said sharply, "Why do you people in the West say bad things about Prophet Mohammed, peace and blessing of Allah be upon him?"

Jacob was slightly taken aback, but he managed to say with a smile, "I never did."

"But some people in the West always do," replied the man with the turban.

"Mohammed, peace and blessing of Allah be upon him, was a prophet like every other prophet," the man with thick black hair said. "We believe in Issa (Jesus), and respect him as our prophet, too. We Muslims believe in all prophets, from Adam to the last one, Mohammed, peace and blessing of Allah be upon him."

Jacob shrugged his shoulders, trying to think of what to say. The man with the thick black hair asked, "Don't the Westerners have other things to do besides insulting our prophet, saying that he was only a poet?" Jacob did not know what he meant.

The man in the turban looked at his friend, and told him with his eyes to change his tone of voice and to be friendly. Then he looked at Jacob and said, "Prophet Mohammed was the same as Issa and Musa (Moses). Like Musa and Issa, God sent the same archangel Gabriel to tell him that he was the chosen one."

The man then recited from the Holy Koran, first in Arabic, and then in Dari,

> Gabriel said, and Prophet Mohammed, peace and blessing of Allah be upon him, repeated after him, 'Proclaim in the name of your Lord who is the creator and cherisher of all. He created man out of a clot of blood. Proclaim the glory of your Lord who is the most bountiful. He taught man the use of his pen. Taught him what he did not know.' (96:1–5)

The man in the white hat carried the story forward. "Mohammed, peace and blessing of Allah be upon him, was not a poet. He was chosen as our guide to lead us into the right path. This is how the first revelation extolled the power of the pen."

Jacob listened attentively, inclining his head politely. When the three guys had stopped talking, he asked. "Is there anything in the Koran that talks about freedom of worship, that anyone can choose his or her religion?

"Yes, there is," the man in the black turban said triumphantly. Then he recited in Arabic,

Let there be no compulsion in religion, for this is the truth, which stands out from error. Whoever rejects evil and believes in God shall grasp the most dependable handle. (2:256)

Before Jacob could ask another question, the man in the white hat recited another verse in Arabic,

Tell the disbelievers: I do not worship what you worship, nor do you worship what I worship. I will not worship what you worship, nor will you worship what I worship. To you, your religion, and to me, mine. (10:1–6)

Jacob moved his head as a sign of agreement. The man in the white hat said, "We have one request from you."

"Sure!" Jacob said agreeably.

"Please tell your people when you go back to the West, do not insult Mohammed, peace and blessing of Allah be upon him. He was a prophet like other prophets. We don't insult any of the prophets. From Adam to Issa we respect them as we respect Mohammed, peace and blessing of Allah be upon him, and believe in their books, but we follow our book, the Holy Koran."

"I will be happy to deliver your message," Jacob told them.

They shook hands with Jacob with friendly smiles on their faces, and walked away. As they went, the man with thick black hair said, "Enjoy our beautiful country."

"I will," Jacob replied warmly.

∽

From the Jumaa Mosque, we walked the short distance to the Citadel where we would be performing the next day. We wanted to make sure that everything was ready, without any of the surprises we had encountered in Mazar. Arash Boostani, the engineer overseeing the restoration of the Citadel for the Aga Khan Trust for Culture, had arranged everything. All we had to do was show his people where we wanted the chairs.

Arash gave us tea in his office in a low workshop building in front of the massive walls that had been under construction when Alexander of Macedon arrived in 330 BCE. He showed us some plans of the Citadel, indicating what parts had already been reconstructed and which would be next. Then he gave us a quick tour. We walked through a huge gate, and climbed up to an inner fort that sits at the highest point of the Citadel like an eagle's nest over Herat.

In one direction, we could see the Jumaa Mosque, with its minarets and high-arched *iwans*, where it rose up out of the Old City, whose neat grid-like streets stretched before us. In the other direction, we had a clear view of the remnants of a palace and *madrassa* complex built in the early 1400s by the son of Tamburlaine and his wife, Gowhar Shad. Together, they had fostered in Herat a golden age for the arts. Gravity-defying minarets lean in all directions, held erect now by cables. Beyond the minarets were the mountains.

There had been many more minarets, but, a century ago, British military commanders ordered them destroyed, claiming they could be used as cover by the Russians if ever they attacked Herat. The attack never came. The minarets lie in ruins. This is the sad story of Afghan history.

When we got back to the Mawfaq Hotel, no one was there, except for Parwin. The others, she said, had gone to the candy market to buy some sweets and pastries. Herat is famous for its confectionaries. Anyone who goes to Mazar feels obligated to visit the shrine. In Herat, they have to go to the candy market. About half an hour later, the actors arrived with bags filled with all kinds of sweets. We had tea, talked and joked. By then it was dark.

With the show the next day, the plan was to have an early meal and a quiet evening. Nabi Tanha and Shah Mohammed did not come with us. Nabi Tanha had had a fight with Breshna Bahar. Nabi Tanha refused to eat with her, and Shah Mohammed always does what Nabi Tanha does. Of course, the next day they had forgotten whatever had so vexed them the night before.

The rest of us went to the Arghawan Restaurant and sat on raised platforms known as *tapchans* built in alcoves around a rock-pile fountain full of frolicking cement deer, but no water. The girls made fun of the dry fountain. The waiter who served us was very excited to see the actors. A painting of Maryam, the mother of Prophet Issa, hung on one wall.

Later, we all went out to the park that stretches down the centre of the main boulevard along the north side of the Old City. You can still see portions of the thousand-year-old city walls paralleling the park a short distance away. We found some water pipe vendors in the park, and settled in for a relaxing hour of sucking in apple-scented tobacco smoke. It was ironic that in a city with clean air, everyone wanted to breathe smoke.

For the actors, freed from their obligations at home, this was as close to a vacation as some of them had ever known. The concept of 'leisure time' is all but unknown in Afghanistan. The pleasing atmosphere of Herat put everyone in a sweet mood.

Even their cosmic complaints were gentled. The most anyone could find to complain about was the wind. While it is true that every year Herat has one hundred or more days of wind, that night there was hardly a breeze. It caressed everyone's faces, and carried the blue smoke from the pipes to search for the noses of people happy to smell it.

∽

The next day, the actors were displeased with the breakfast that the hotel served. Some of them were extra cranky, because they had stayed up the night before to watch the Soca Warriors of Trinidad and Tobago challenge David Beckham's England team for the World Cup in Germany. Trinidad and Tobago had lost their match, but they had prevented England's millionaire superstars from scoring a single goal until the 83rd minute.

The football fans among us were extolling the team's determination to prevail, even though they had lost the match. This is a concept that every Afghan understands. The actors cheered for Trinidad, even though most of them had never heard of it before. They decided we should have a party to celebrate.

We gave money to Arif and Nazeef and told them to go buy the best food they could find. They brought back a feast of chicken and lamb *kebab* and *qabuli pelau*. Soon, the complaints were replaced by lots of jokes and singing.

∽

We still had several hours before the performance, so we went to the Citadel to take a look at it. Like many historic buildings, it had been closed for at least twenty years. None of the actors had ever been inside it before.

As soon as we got inside its gates, they started running around like kids who had been brought to a nice playground. They were climbing from one tower to the next. From the top, they took photos with beautiful views of Herat spreading below. They were truly amazed by the size of the Citadel, by its elegantly constructed arches and its high walls that looked as if they had been built by giants. They started telling each other heroic tales.

Leila struck a pose in front of a towering column and proclaimed, "There was a queen here. She was the ruler of this place. She had thousands at her disposal, all of them her servants. She used to sit on a chair made of gold and covered with diamonds. With a flicker of a finger, her orders were fulfilled. People feared and loved her. They feared her because she could do anything, and loved her because she was mighty and kind to her people. When she went out, she travelled in splendid style in a horse-drawn carriage escorted by bodyguards of cavalry."

Faisal raised his arms in protest, as if shocked by her pronouncements. "No, it was a man who ruled this place. He had thousands of soldiers waiting for his orders. He was feared throughout the region. Every boy dreamed to be like him one day. He was a legend, the greatest conqueror the world has ever known. He had a ferocious army that blazed across the world, razing cites, torturing and decapitating his enemies. He had poets, philosophers, thinkers, writers, storytell-ers, musicians, and clowns waiting for him to clap his hands and tell them: 'Come.'"

People like that really had lived in this place. Perhaps Leila and Faisal were hearing the whispers of their ghosts.

As the day grew warmer, the actors got tired of exploring. The sun was intense and hot, and the wind was real wind now, not just a breeze. Nabi Tanha suggested that we should go through the script to pass the time. We went inside some rooms that had been offered to us. They had thick mud-brick walls and domes. One led to another; they were all connected to one another without a wall in between. They were very cool.

We sat in a circle, and started. Since all the actors were very confi-dent of their lines and cues now, they put their texts on the ground. Nobody made any mistakes. Nobody was nervous or unhappy. Every-one was very comfortable with one another.

❦

Around 4:00pm, the audience started to arrive. Many of them were women from Herat University. They all came in wearing *burqas* that made them seem to glide rather than walk. Once they were within the Citadel's second set of walls where the seating for the play had been set up, they threw off the *burqas* and became chattering young women, many in designer jeans.

The pleated blue *burqas* were folded, and placed carefully over the backs of their chairs. Many young men showed up as well, most of them also from the university, and most of them wearing stylish western clothes. About two hundred and fifty people attended. With almost half of them women, we finally achieved in Herat one of the goals that had propelled us to do this project.

The show went very smoothly. A few Afghan soldiers who had been appointed to provide our security were so caught up in the play that they came and stood near the platform where the actors did the first scene, and stayed there transfixed until the end of the play. They were probably uneducated, and maybe even illiterate, but Shake-speare's poetry kept them entranced.

We had no tent for the girls to use, so we changed the lines to say that they would have to stay in a caravanserai. We had done the same a few weeks before in Kabul when we were performing in the reconstructed caravanserai at the Bagh-e-Babur. We were learning the art of adapting as we went. The rooms where we had been relaxing became the caravanserai for the performance.

The real star of the show was the Citadel. *Love's Labour's Lost* takes place in front of a castle. The Foundation for Culture and Civil Society had provided us with a beautiful garden and a palatial house, but it was not a castle. At the Bagh-e-Babur we had stone battlements that looked like a castle, but, in fact, they were not a castle. Here in the Citadel of Herat, we had the Qala Ikhtyaruddin, a castle that was truly a real castle!

Line upon line of yellow brick arches rose behind our stage. In every direction, high stone towers dominated the view. Walls surrounded us, and a moat surrounded them. This was a castle. As the play progressed and the sun dipped, the yellow brick walls turned to a fiery gold.

The audience listened to everything very carefully. Many of them were studying literature. Most said that this was the first play they had ever seen. At the first jokes, they smiled, and looked at one another. They were not sure they were allowed to laugh.

When the girls entered in their brightly-coloured costumes, many of the women sat up straighter to get a better view. The jokes began to get bigger laughs. By the time the boys had revealed to each other that they had all fallen in love, the audience had lost its inhibitions and was laughing out loud. Then came the scene with the Indian songs, and – as we now fully expected – they all went crazy. As they had in Mazar, all the boys but Shah Mohammed chose to wear their black T-shirts with their *dhotis*.

Not one thing went wrong in that show. It probably was the best performance the actors had ever given.

～

Afterward, Nabi Tanha talked to some Herati journalists. He spoke about the power of theatre, saying, "This was in our culture once. It is not new to us, and we want to see more. Slowly, slowly, we have to take a step. Things will take time to change."

Jacob Baynham chatted with a young Afghan woman who spoke fluent English. She told him: "This is the first time a woman has been on stage in Herat. Now more will follow, because it won't be taboo anymore." Insh'allah. But a few weeks later, a bomb went off at Herat University protesting the education of women. Four young women were killed. We grimly wondered if any of them had been among those who had come to see our play.

When the actors had finished speaking with several journalists who had come to interview them, they rushed toward the domed dressing room where cakes and cookies were arranged for them. Nabi Tanha poured tea into a plastic cup, and sipped some. He spat it out right away and said, "This tea smells like burning plastic."

Shah Mohammed said, "It is not the tea. It is the plastic teacups that make it smell like that."

"Aga Khan's wealth is all over the world," Nabi Tanha railed, "yet he serves us tea in plastic cups." He put his cup on the table. By now we knew that when Nabi Tanha was fussing, he was happy. We watched him as he ate some cake and cookies, talked to the actors, and absent-mindedly picked up his cup again and took a sip. He forcefully spat it back into the cup, and said, "Why do I keep reaching for this smelly plastic tea?"

"Because you are thirsty," Shah Mohammed said with mock solicitude. Everybody laughed except Nabi Tanha.

"Find me some water," Nabi Tanha ordered imperiously to no one in particular. No one paid any attention to him.

There were parts of *Love's Labour's Lost* that we would miss. And parts that we would not.

૭

That night nobody was having fights with anybody, so everybody went back to the same restaurant, the Arghawan, to enjoy its good food, and to laugh at its dry fountain with the cement deer. Later we went again to the water pipes in the park.

And then, quite unexpectedly, we had a *shehr jangi*, a poetry battle.

It started when Nabi Tanha blew a huge puff of smoke into the darkening sky and recited one of his most poetic speeches from *Love's Labour's Lost*. Perhaps he was expecting applause. He deserved it. He recited poetry with exceptional skill.

Instead, Leila responded by reciting a sonnet by Rumi in a competitive tone. Her selection started with the last letter of Nabi Tanha's poem, which was a loud and clear message that she was challenging him to come back with something better.

Nabi Tanha's faithful lieutenant Shah Mohammed stepped in for his Commander and recited a two-verse poem that started with the last letter of Leila's poem. Now, if anyone had doubted it, we were having an all-out contest, and that the boys were pitted against the girls.

Very quickly, the stakes were raised. It was no longer good enough just to recite a poem that started with the last letter of the previous one. If one of the boys recited a two- or four-verse poem about love, one of the girls had to reply with a poem about the deeper meaning of love, devotion or being loyal. And so it went for hours, shifting from love poems to spiritual poems, to epic poems, to patriotic poems, back to love poems, and so on.

For example, Arif recited a couplet by Hafiz against the girls, while he looked all of them in the eye:

O beloved, I promise I will never turn my face away from you again,
Even if you stone me, or with curses drive me away.

Leila jumped in with a couplet by the same poet that started with the Dari equivalent of the letter "Y":

You are the messenger of the mystery, and now I know I'm on the right path,
So, do not give me orders, but urge me gently on.

Everybody cheered, "Bravo, Leila jan!" Faisal then joined the fight and recited a couplet against Leila and all the girls with a poem that started with the letter "N":

Not even a hundred beautiful women could lure me from this place,

Could ambush my heart with an army of idols reeking of perfume.

The boys shouted, "Bravo, Faisal jan!" Breshna Bahar then took it upon herself to avenge the girls. She recited a four-verse poem from Rumi against Faisal and all the boys. It started with the letter "E":

Eternity waits behind the transparent door
Of each moment. Love the beloved, and that door
Swings open: Eternity enters, pouring the wine
No one who drinks can ever recover from.

All the girls yelled, "Bravo, Breshna jan!" Now the contest was slowly shifting to spiritual poems. One of the boys had to recite a poem starting with the letter "M", but not about love, but rather about something deeper. Nabi Tanha was fastest:

My heart has run on water all day,
And will pray on Sinai all night,
Yet some say, 'No one can walk on water,
Or climb up Sinai without feet.'

All the boys cheered, "Bravo, Nabi jan! Up until then, Parwin had been quietly listening, except for bursts of her melodic laughter. Unexpectedly she recited:

They prattle of 'balance,' of 'moderation,' of 'decorum,'
I wrote on one of the doors in secret:
'You think you know, you died long ago;
You think you see? Reason ate your eyes.'

The girls clapped and said, "Bravo, Parwin jan!" The boys looked at one another for several moments, but no one could come up with something as strong as what Parwin had just recited, even though they all had poems they could recite that started with the letter "S". But Parwin's poem had been a heavyweight, and none of the boys could find one its equal. When the pause lasted for more than half a minute, first one of the girls, then all of them, started shouting:

"Qais, you must be the judge. Yes, Qais is the judge. Qais jan, they are too slow; you must say that we are the winners." I did.

Gloomy looks conquered the boys' faces. They had fought hard, and had been tripped up by soft-spoken Parwin. They demanded a rematch. I had to start it with a new poem, and it did not matter what it was about. I chose my favourite verses by Maulana Jala-e-Din Mohammed Balkhi, known to the world as Rumi:

Come, come, whoever you are, wanderer, worshiper, lover of leaving:
It doesn't matter –
Ours is not a caravan of despair,
but one of endless joy.
Even if you have broken your vows a hundred times –
Come, come, yet again, come!

And with those sweet words of spiritual invitation and ecstasy, the battle commenced anew. By then it was past midnight, but the competition continued for another three and a half hours. All of the boys and the girls were sleepy, but nobody wanted to stop as long as the other side was winning. We finally called a truce, with the score tied.

Jacob Baynham, who had sat quiet and spellbound while the battle raged, later noted with amazement that "although literacy rates in Afghanistan are low, few literate young people in America could claim to command a fraction of the cultural heritage that these young Afghans shared."

The poetry contest kept the actors busy, and gave them no chance to complain about anything. We enjoyed listening to their poetry. And they all knew how to recite it beautifully. If they had kept copies of all the poems they recited in the competition from beginning to end, their poems would have made a very thick book.

Everybody went to the hotel to catch a few hours of sleep. But that did not mean the contest ended there. It continued the next day as soon as everyone woke up. While we were having breakfast, it erupted again. A few of the waiters joined as they served us *naan*, yoghurt and tea. No one won.

Again a truce was called as we went to pack our bags to go to the airport. But in the terminal, as we were waiting for the plane, it started again. A few passengers joined. Still, no one won. The contest did not stop in the plane; it continued at 30,000 feet. No one won.

We reached Kabul at the end of the day, and it continued all the way to the baggage claim. A guy who had arrived from Kandahar a few minutes ahead of us, and who was also waiting for his baggage, joined the actors as soon as he realised they were in a poetry battle. He was fast, and his poems were sharp, but unfortunately every poem he recited, we had already heard. He had no way of knowing that the contest was by then nearly seventeen hours old with no repeats.

The actors made fun of him for reciting verses they had already used. He offered one poem after another, more than ten of them. But no sooner had he recited the opening verse, than the actors in one loud voice exclaimed mockingly, "Old one!"

He laughed, and said, "You people are way too far ahead of me. We can go on like this for hours. Goodbye!" He put the strap of his bag on his shoulder, and stepped to one side as the baggage belt began moving. As he did, Shah Mohammed quickly recited a poem to jab him for not being able to compete:

The beauty of this poem is beyond words.
Do you need a guide to experience the heat of the sun?

Everybody laughed, including the man from Kandahar. He said, "Good one!" as he waited for his bags to arrive. Shy Kabir suddenly recited another one to poke more fun at him:

If you wake up tomorrow with headache or hangover,
Drink more wine, and chase this discomfort away.

The man smiled slightly, but we could see that he was no longer enjoying this. Then Arif lobbed another one, which made everybody roar with laughter, except for the man, who was becoming very embarrassed. It had stopped being a joke for him. Arif recited:

O fool, do something, so you won't just stand there looking dumb.
If you are not travelling and on the road, how can you call yourself a guide?

The baggage arrived. The Kandahari man grabbed his, and quickly disappeared.

As soon as we were out of the terminal, the contest started again. Daoud had come to the airport to pick us up. When he let the girls off at their homes, they said their goodbyes with poems. The contest continued. No one won.

The next day we met at the Foundation. The battle began again. Corinne wanted to hear all the details of our performance in Herat. When she asked the actors about the show, they answered by pelting poems at the other side. Corinne wanted to know what was being said. We told her it was a poetry contest, that it had been going since two nights before, and that it was not easy to translate the verses. They were coming too fast.

In the end, 'Qais the Judge' had to announce that both parties were equal. No one won. Everyone was upset by that. In Afghanistan, the only thing worse than losing is ending in a tie. They complained loudly, but they know that in our country a judge can do anything he wants.

In truth, it was better for both parties not to have the other the clear winner. If the boys were declared the winners, the girls would only want to challenge them again. And if the girls had won, the boys would be forced to challenge them. It was a question of honour. And it could go on like that for days.

And that is how our production of *Love's Labour's Lost* ended: on a wave of sublime poetry and fierce competition.

Thank you, Corinne. Thank you, Malcolm Jardine and Richard Weyers of the British Council and the people of the United Kingdom who provided the funds. Thank you, Norbert Spitz of the Goethe Institut and the people of Germany who provided its funds. Thank you, Robert Kluijver and Timor Hakimyar and the entire Foundation for Culture and Civil Society. Thank you, Jolyon Leslie and the Aga Khan Trust for Culture. Thank you, Shahla Nawabi for your exquisite costumes. Thank you, Rahim Walizada and Mujeeb Siddiqi for your magnificent carpets. Thank you, all the Afghan and international journalists who told our story. Thank you, Vincent Desforges and Frank Bouis for your generous expressions of confidence in what we were doing.

And thank you, William Shakespeare, for writing an Afghan play, even if you did not know that you had, and for giving us jokes that still make people laugh more than four hundred years after you wrote them.

"So now, you that way: we this way."

25

Curtain

Kabul. December, 2009.

Love's Labour's Lost had ended, but the journey that had begun with it for the actors continued.

Arif Bahonar, along with some other members of the Groupe Aftab, was invited by Ariane Mnouchkine to study with her in Paris over the next several summers.

Nabi Tanha was tapped by Hollywood producers to play a featured role in the film of Khaled Hosseini's acclaimed novel, *The Kite Runner*.

Corinne returned each summer to Kabul for the next three years, but with a different play this time, one written by a Frenchman named Fabrice Melquiot. It was called *Sisters*, and was only for the girls. Corinne wanted to give the girls a chance to try out a different kind of acting. The play was based on stories from the girls' own lives.

Breshna Bahar and her daughter Wazhma were among the cast, which also included Marina Gulbahari. Ariane arranged for them to perform *Sisters* in Paris at her complex at the Cartoucherie, and subsequently invited Wazhma to remain in Paris as part of the Groupe Aftab.

During the six weeks that the girls spent in Paris living in quaint 19th century horse-drawn caravans amid the lush greenery of the Bois de Vincennes, they made a startling discovery: they were all desperately homesick for Kabul.

❧

As the girls were preparing to take *Sisters* to Paris, a terrible thing happened.

Parwin's husband heard a loud knocking at his door one night. After he and Parwin had been forced to leave his family's house during *Love's Labour's Lost*, they had found a small house of their own, far out from the city in a neighbourhood called Shooda, near a large cemetery. The rude remarks about Parwin's work as an actress continued to be made within her husband's family. But in their new home, Parwin and her husband did not have to listen to them every night.

Whoever was knocking started shouting as well. They ignored him. The same guy came back the next evening at around five o'clock, and shouted for her husband to come out and meet him.

"Though it was getting dark, my husband said it would be better if he went to talk to him," she recounted afterwards. "He did not come back right away, as I had expected. In fact, after one hour, he still had not come back. By now it was completely dark, and we had no electricity for lights. I was becoming very scared. I tried calling him, but his phone was off."

At eight o'clock, she heard three shots. She started to shake. She was too frightened to scream.

"I couldn't go out, because I was very scared," said Parwin. "I was alone with my kids, and there was no other man in my family. I could feel that something had happened, but I didn't know what. My children started crying, and asking where their dad was. I couldn't do anything, so I just said that he would come. I locked the door of the house, and stayed awake all night. I was afraid that someone might come for me and the children."

In the morning, she could hear other voices in the street. Through her window, she saw a policeman come through her gate, and walk across the garden toward the house. She started to pray as she opened the door to him.

He addressed her formally in a quiet voice. "*Hamshira*," which means 'sister.' "I must tell you something, but my mouth does not wish to make these words." Parwin could hold back the tears no longer. The children started to cry as well, not knowing what was happening. A neighbour's wife and sister came running into the house, wailing and screaming and praying loudly.

Outside, across the street from the house at the edge of the cemetery, Parwin's husband lay dead, the blood from a gaping wound in his face now dried in the dust.

Parwin and her children fled from the house that same day. She and her husband had tried so hard not to upset anyone with her work. They thought they could outrun the gossip. She went to her sister's house for that night, and then to a different house the next night, and to still a different house the night after. Her husband's brothers took away his body to Khost for burial, and organised the funeral there. She never saw him again, nor had a chance to say goodbye.

In the weeks that followed, Parwin and the children fled to Pakistan where they thought they would be safe. Meanwhile, Corinne in Paris went into overdrive, seeking assistance from the UN High Commission for Refugees, from the French and Canadian Embassies in Pakistan. She made phone calls and sent e-mails by the dozens. She was relentless in her efforts.

She was helped immensely by a Canadian theatre director, Christopher Morris, who had been in Kabul some months earlier looking for an Afghan actress for a play he was planning to direct at his Human Cargo Theatre in Toronto. He had met Parwin, and was deeply moved when he had heard about the pressure she was under from her husband's family. Now he was utterly horrified by what had happened. He started working as tirelessly as Corinne to get Parwin out of danger.

Months of e-mails, phone calls, pleas to bureaucrats and diplomats followed. Christina Lamb, a journalist from *The Sunday Times* in London who had published a much-acclaimed book about Afghanistan titled *The Sewing Circles of Herat* wrote a feature story about Parwin that captured the agony that she and her children were enduring.

One day, two men whom Parwin did not recognise showed up at the house where they were hiding in Islamabad. They threatened her and the children. Again she fled, first to a mosque, and then to a women's shelter.

It took a year of unyielding efforts by Corinne in Paris and

Christopher Morris in Canada, but finally Parwin and the kids were given UN refugee documents and entry visas to Canada.

Odile Jouanneau, the wife of the French Ambassador in Islamabad, was very kind to Parwin. She visited Parwin and the children several times, and encouraged her husband to mention Parwin's case informally with the Canadian Ambassador in an effort to get the paperwork processed a little faster. On the day that Parwin and her children left Pakistan for Canada, she drove them to the airport.

They landed in Toronto, exhausted and terrified, but eagerly welcomed by the group of Canadians whom Christopher Morris had gathered to help them get resettled.

Six months later, the children were speaking English, and Parwin was beginning not to panic when she heard a knock at the door.

∿

London. December, 2010.

In late 2010, Corinne was contacted by Shakespeare's Globe Theatre in London. To coincide with the London Olympics in 2012, The Globe planned to present all of Shakespeare's plays in languages other than English. They were calling it *Globe to Globe*. It was part of the *World Shakespeare Festival* being organised by the Royal Shakespeare Company.

The British Council was willing to underwrite the cost of bringing a group of actors from Afghanistan. They asked Corinne if she might direct her *Love's Labour's Lost* troupe in a different play in May 2012. They proposed *Richard II*.

"Afghans don't do tragedy," Corinne told them.

"*The Comedy of Errors*?" they asked.

"Let's talk," she replied.

The End

Authors' Note

We very much wanted Corinne Jaber to join us as a co-writer of this book, and were greatly disappointed when she declined our many invitations, noting that she may want to write her own account of *Shakespeare in Kabul* some day. We hope she does, and wish her well with it.

Much appreciation to Dr. Irena R. Makaryk, the Vice Dean of Graduate Studies at the University of Ottawa, whose presentation on our *Love's Labour's Lost* at the International Shakespeare Congress in Stratford-upon-Avon in 2008, and her scholarly article about it published from Warsaw in 2011 in the journal *Multicultural Shakespeare: Translation, Appropriation and Performance* first made us aware of the widespread interest in *Shakespeare in Kabul*.

Special thanks to Laurence E. Landrigan and Meaghan Luthin for their much-valued editing. Additional thanks to Christine Shields who made many helpful and needed things happen in her quiet and effective way.

Profound gratitude to Barbara Schwepcke and her team at Haus Publishing – notably Harry Hall, Aida Bahrami and Ilse Schwepcke – for their enthusiastic embrace of *Shakespeare in Kabul*.

And an appreciation beyond our ability to express to Elspeth Cochrane who never stopped looking for ways to bring our *Love's Labour's Lost* to London, and, failing that, did much to get this chronicle of *Shakespeare in Kabul* into print.